# *Mighty Rough Times, I Tell You*

Written by Andrea Sutcliffe

*Touring the Shenandoah Valley Backroads*

Other Titles in the *Real Voices, Real History Series*™

*On Jordan's Stormy Banks*, edited by Andrew Waters

*We Lived in a Little Cabin in the Yard*, edited by Belinda Hurmence

*Before Freedom, When I Just Can Remember*,
edited by Belinda Hurmence

*My Folks Don't Want Me to Talk about Slavery*,
edited by Belinda Hurmence

# Mighty Rough Times, I Tell You

## Personal Accounts of Slavery in Tennessee



EDITED BY ANDREA SUTCLIFFE

JOHN F. BLAIR, PUBLISHER
*Winston-Salem, North Carolina*

*Published by John F. Blair, Publisher*



*The paper in this book meets the guidelines for permanence and durability of the Committee on Production Guidelines for Book Longevity of the Council on Library Resources.*

Library of Congress Cataloging-in-Publication Data
Mighty rough times, I tell you: personal accounts of slavery in Tennessee / edited by Andrea Sutcliffe.
p. cm.—(Real voices, real history series)
ISBN 0-89587-226-9 (alk. paper)
1. Slaves—Tennessee—Biography. 2. Slaves—Tennessee—Social conditions—19th century. 3. Afro-Americans—Tennessee—Interviews. 4. Afro-Americans—Tennessee—Social conditions—19th century. 5. Tennessee—Biography. 6. Tennessee—Race relations. I. Sutcliffe, Andrea. II. Series.
E445.T3 M46 2000
976.8'00496073'0092—dc21
[B] 00-064191

*Cover photo from the Library of Congress,*
*U.S. Farm Security Administration Collection (LC-USF 34-17494-E)*

*Design by Debra Long Hampton*

# *Contents*

* *WPA narratives*

## *Introduction*

The stories in this volume are first-person accounts of slavery as recalled by former slaves living in Tennessee in the late 1920s and 1930s. Most were in their eighties and nineties at the time they were interviewed, and a few had even passed the century mark. Although their recollections were of events that took place when they were children or teenagers and thus may not be entirely reliable, their stories provide vivid and disturbing images of everyday slave life on Tennessee farms and plantations in the mid-1800s.

The idea of interviewing slaves about their experiences dates to the 1760s, when abolitionists began to publish slave narratives as a way to educate the public about the horrors of slavery. Many of the selections in this book were the result of a project of the Social Sciences Department at Fisk University in 1929 and 1930. In 1934, during the Great Depression, one of the Fisk project workers suggested that the Federal Emergency

Relief Administration hire unemployed white-collar blacks to undertake similar projects in two other states. Some 250 interviews were conducted in Indiana and Kentucky but were never published. Two years later, the Works Progress Administration (WPA) picked up on the idea and directed Federal Writers' Project teams in South Carolina, Virginia, Georgia, and Florida to begin interviewing former slaves living in their states. The project soon expanded to additional states. Interviewers, most of whom were white, were given lists of questions and told how to record the interviews to reflect the spoken black dialects.

By the time the WPA project ended in 1938, some two thousand interviews, representing about 2 percent of the ex-slave population in the United States at the time, had been completed and transcribed. Ten thousand pages of typewritten material were sent to the Library of Congress, which organized the collection and published it in seventeen volumes under the title *Slave Narratives: A Folk History of Slavery in the United States from Interviews with Former Slaves*. In the 1970s, historian George P. Rawick compiled not only the narratives deposited with the Library of Congress but also the hundreds that had never been sent to Washington, which he found in various state, university, and historical society collections all over the country. Rawick's series, which reprints the entire Fisk project in volumes 18 and 19, is entitled *The American Slave: A Composite Autobiography*.

Only 26 WPA narratives were included in the Library

of Congress collection for Tennessee. Most states produced many more than that (South Carolina, for example, had 284). In his introduction to *The American Slave*, Rawick offers no explanation for the small number of narratives for Tennessee other than to state that several of them were not included because they may have been "fraudulent," appearing to be copies of previously published material. More than sixty years later, all we can surmise is that perhaps the Federal Writers' Project team for Tennessee was not well staffed, or that the project coordinators felt that the interviews conducted by Fisk University had sufficiently recorded the experience of slavery in Tennessee.

Readers who are familiar with WPA slave narratives from other states may notice a distinct difference in both the tone and content of many of the accounts in this collection. In particular, the interviewees in the Fisk University project were more outspoken, on the whole, than the WPA subjects about the cruelties they endured under slavery. One possible reason is that the Fisk interviews were conducted by Ophelia Settle Egypt, a Howard University graduate who was working for Dr. Charles Johnson, a professor in Fisk's Social Sciences Department. Both were black, and it is possible that the former slaves felt comfortable relating their experiences to a black professional woman who encouraged them to speak about their experiences, good and bad. (Years later, Ms. Egypt was instrumental in opening the first family-planning clinic in southeast Washington, D.C.) By contrast, most of the WPA interviewers were white women from the middle and upper classes in the communities where the interviews were conducted. No doubt many had ties to local charitable and governmental organizations that Depression-era blacks relied on for help. All of the former slaves appear to have been struggling to get by, and fear of retribution may have played a role as they answered the interviewers' questions. Even one of the Fisk subjects asks, "Say, is there any danger in this talk? If so, I want to take back everything I said."

Another possible reason for the relative mildness of many of the WPA interviews, as Rawick explains in his introduction to *The American Slave*, was censorship on the part of some of the state project directors. It appears that in at least a few cases, certain narratives were deemed "too hot" and thus were never sent to the central program office in Washington. Rawick also mentions that some narratives were apparently "toned down" at the state level.

Whether WPA or Fisk, the narratives in this volume vary in how they portray the trials of daily life under the master and mistress. It appears that a few slaves may have been treated fairly well—but only relatively speaking. It is important to read between the lines. Many claim their masters were good to them but later mention frequent whippings, often saying they were painful but deserved. Others take a relative view: "My old marster was right good to us—that is, he wasn't as mean as some of them was." One ex-slave, the mulatto son of his master's son, doesn't mince words about his masters but then quickly seems to regret it: "If I had my way with them, all I would like to have is a chopping block and chop every one of their heads off. Of course, I don't hate them; that is good." Almost every narrative makes matter-of-fact mention of daily or weekly whippings, sexual abuse, punishments for trying to learn to read or write, the inability to worship freely, and cruel separations of family members. As one former slave puts it, "We didn't know nothing else but slavery—never thought of nothing else. I just know I belonged to the man who provided for me, and I had to take whatever he give me."

Tennessee was not a large slaveholding state compared with others in the South. The number of slaves in the state grew from 3,417 in 1790 to more than 275,000 by the time the Civil War ended in 1865. By then, blacks represented one-fourth of the state's population. Most Tennesseans were not slaveholders—fewer than one family in five owned slaves in 1860. Interestingly, as Caleb Patterson describes in his 1922 book, *The Negro in Tennessee, 1780–1865*, Tennessee was a leading state in attempts to abolish slavery before 1830. By 1827, there were 130 such groups in the United States, 25 of which were based in Tennessee. Until 1834, free black men had the right to vote in the state. Then the tide began to turn against abolition because of growing concerns over slave rebellions and riots in neighboring states. Although the 7,300 free blacks in Tennessee around 1860 still had some legal rights, they weren't allowed to associate with slaves (for fear they would encourage them to flee), and most whites refused to mix with free blacks in society or give them jobs. Many free blacks supported their families by performing odd jobs. Some were lucky enough to own small farms.

Readers should keep in mind that the economic lives of most former slaves did not improve a great deal after 1865. In fact, several mention that times were better "in the old days" because they didn't have to face the problems of obtaining food, clothing, and shelter. Especially tragic are those who mention their inability to receive old-age pensions, military pensions, or some other form of government relief. Even so, their comments should not be taken to mean that they thought slavery was preferable to freedom, as advocates of slavery have often claimed. In fact, the interviewees say that even though times were hard, "I would die fighting rather than be a slave again" and "I'd rather be out of slavery than in, all the time."

Besides providing a highly personal look at the American tragedy that was slavery, many of the interviews also recount important events in Tennessee history, including the Battle of Nashville and the Confederate massacre of black Union soldiers at Fort Pillow. Places and events in Nashville in particular are frequently mentioned. Some interviewees describe being put on the block in the city's slave-trading yards, watching Union soldiers march through town, seeing the construction of the state capitol, riding in segregated streetcars, attending some of the first classes at Fisk University, and hearing about (and in one case actually participating in) Fisk's famous Jubilee Singers, who toured the world to raise money to keep their school open. Several mention witnessing or hearing about a black man named Eph Grizzard, who was lynched in Nashville for his involvement with a white woman; this was clearly in response to a standard interview question.

For this book, I selected thirty-six of the most interesting interviews recorded by the WPA (indicated by asterisks in the table of contents) and the Fisk University projects. All the ex-slaves whose accounts are included here were at least ten years old at the time the Civil War ended. I edited the narratives for readability by removing most of the black dialect—much of it excessive—recorded especially by the WPA interviewers. I also rearranged paragraphs for better chronological flow, omitted redundant or extraneous information, and shortened lengthy narratives. I did not correct grammar, and in some cases I retained certain commonplace variants—for example, *master, marster*, and *marse*—that were consistently used. In several instances, I have provided explanatory information and definitions of unfamiliar words in brackets. When the names of the narrators were available, I included them, but many of the Fisk-interviewed subjects unfortunately remain anonymous. Finally, because all the Fisk narratives had titles, I created titles for the WPA narratives as well, for the sake of consistency.

Many thanks are due the librarians who took time to

help me on this project. They include Zelli Fischetti and Linda Belford at the Western Historical Manuscripts Collection at the University of Missouri–St. Louis; Sally R. Polhemus at the McClung Historical Collection of the Knox County library system; William B. Eigelsbach at the University of Tennessee libraries; and Beth M. Howse at the Fisk University library. In addition, the librarians in the Prints and Photographs Reading Room of the Library of Congress were knowledgeable and helpful.

# Mighty Rough Times, I Tell You

❋

# Mighty Rough Times, I Tell You

Well, ladies, I can't tell you nothing 'cept I was treated pretty bad, knocked and kicked around like I was a mule. They would tie you up to a tree, tie your hands down, and whip you. They was awful mean in Georgia. You was never allowed to have a piece of paper to look at. They would whip you for that because they didn't want you to learn anything. When they would whip you, they would tear your back all to pieces. Child, they didn't care for you. We had to stand in fear of them; we had no protection. They would take your clothes off and whip you like you was no more than mules.

The man who owned us was right clever to us. He give my mother a little patch to raise cotton, and when he would sell it he would always give her the money. Heap of them was too lazy to work a patch. He would give her a half-day on Saturday to work her crop. On moonlight nights, we would work it, too. Every family had a cabin to theirself. Hogs was wild; they just roved about in the woods trying to find something to eat. It was a mighty poor country. There was plenty of grapes, plums, and watermelons.

You would always have to ask Marster and Mistress every time you wanted to do anything at all. At Christmastime, they would give you something—shoes, hat, and one thing and another. Some would do it, and some wouldn't. When we wanted to have a dance, we had to ask Marster. They would have a fiddler, and we would tromp around mighty.

I was in the Civil War. Mighty rough times, I tell you. My marster sold me. I was in Georgia, then they brought me to Tennessee. I was on the Northern side. The man that bought me brought me from Atlanta to Knoxville. Right at the Knoxville branch, the Yankees met us and made him give me up, so he lost me. I got a discharge, all right, but after the war I was met one night out in the woods, and some robbers robbed me of all the money I had, which was two dollars, and took my discharge papers. I never thought much about it then, but I have never been able to get a pension on account of not having them papers. Several people have tried for me, but I never could tell what regiment I was with. The regiment was from Wisconsin; I remember that all right. And I remember two names of officers; they were Lieutenant Parker and Lieutenant Hughes.

I am eighty-seven years old. The year the Civil War commenced, I was a fifteen-year-old boy. I left 'long about chopping cotton time. The man who sold me was a speculator in slaves. Buy them just like mules. The Yankees took up I don't know how many boys. I waited on two officers. I kept their clothes clean, boots shined, and would bring water. I was standing right 'side of them when they give the discharge papers out, and I would be all right now if I coulda just kept them papers. But I just never was able to get on to getting anything. A old lady in Gallatin told me she was going to write about it for me, but I knowed the old heifer wasn't going to do it. One old man in Gallatin, 'fore I come down here, told me he got three thousand dollars and said I sure ought to got something out of it.

When the Civil War commenced, Marster went and stayed two months, but it rained so much he come back. The man who bought me, the Yankees cut him off at Knoxville. That's how I got to Tennessee.

I reckon my marster had something like fifteen or sixteen grown people on his place. Some of them had a hundred men on their farm at once. They would see children and give them candy. If they looked healthy, they would buy them and raise them up. They would look at them and say, "That's a mighty fine nigger." Mighty few of them had marsters that would treat them right. The niggers was mighty glad to have the Yankees take them; they wanted to get out from under that rough treatment. Georgia was about the meanest place in the world. They would knock and kick you around just like you was dogs.

During the war, when it was time for soldiers to kill a man, twelve of them would have guns, and one would be loaded, and that way none of them would know which one did the killing.

Some of the soldiers would be one side, and if things

got too hot for him he would go over on the other side.

Once we was trying to get to a little town. Men was laying out on the battlefield like cornstalks. We was in a little place called Lowden. The niggers come down with the cannons. Little bullets was flying through the woods. Niggers was standing on that hill. One man went back and said, "Hell done broke loose in Georgia." You could hear men all over the battlefield crying, "Water, water, somebody please give me water." The ambulance would come and get them and try to do something for them, but they couldn't got them fast enough. It was terrible. That was the bloodiest war I ever saw. I believe gunpowder made them mean. They didn't bit more mind shooting you down than they did a partridge.

# They Had Whipping Day Every Thursday

Name unknown

Oh, zam! It's too much of my life to tell it all today.

Well, I were born on Thursday, at seven and a half o'clock in the morning, 1850. There was two of us born in the same house, and the one that was to be born first would get five dollars' reward; I got the reward. Well, you see, I kept the five dollars until I was thirteen years old, in 1863, then I spent that five dollars for five pounds of bacon. Yes'm, I was coming from Tennessee. Yes'm, we was hungry. We was hoboing, you know. We went in a wheat field and fried that bacon and ate it. You know, it was about that same time that there was measles and mumps sweeping the country, and folks was dying ten at a time. They couldn't build coffins fast enough.

Slavery? Well, during slavery, they had whipping day every Thursday. Yes'm, every Thursday was when you got your beating. They had men hired to do the whipping. Everybody got one on Thursday, whether you had been bad or not during the week. They had a log, and they would tie your hands together and tie you to the log, a hand and arm on each side of the log, and whip you. My father ran off and stayed in the woods about a year to keep from taking them whippings. Yes'm, they finally caught him, and the ole marster told him he was going to sell him to the ole nigger seller, and he would take him south. But the war broke out, and the ole nigger seller never did get to come by. The war was pretty hot along about then, and finally my pappy come back of his own accord and joined the Yankee army. Yes'm, it wasn't nothin' but that whipping day that made him run away from home.

Well, we slaves worked every day in the week from sunup to eleven and twelve at night sometime, 'specially in the summer nights. We worked in the fields all the light hours, plowing and planting and such like, then at nights we would shell corn for the fowls and do other things. When the moon shine some nights, we would work in the fields all night. Well, our ole marster was called one of the best marsters in the county. He had five hundred darkies. Everybody had enough to eat. There wasn't no other family of people what done work like we done, 'cause, you see, we was well fed and clothed and everything. We did real farm work—good work, I mean.

I was a house slave. I slept under the stairway in the closet. I was sorta Mistress' pet, you know. We house slaves thought we was better'n the others what worked in the field.

We really was raised a little different, you know. Fact is, I kinda think I'm better'n most folks now. Yes'm, we was raised. They—that is, the field hands—wasn't. They would steal the pigs. I would help them out, too. I never would steal, but if they tell me to say some certain thing I would always do it, you know. My ole mistress was a high-toned woman. She had a kinda liking for all the poor little nigger slaves on the farm. She kinda took to 'em, you know, and mothered and raised 'em like. That's the way she done me, too, and I is still bred like she taught.

Well, the slaves used to have meetings—two weeks' meeting after the tobacco season were over. Sometime there would be a white preacher and sometime a colored preacher. Well, since I have learned exactly what preaching is, I realizes, you know, that they really couldn't preach, but it were good enough in them days, I reckon. Yes'm, they used to get up in the pulpit, these here old preachers, and holler and say, "Oh, the Heaven above and Hell below, run, run, run, sinner." We would have meeting and turn the pots down to keep the sound from the white folks.

Well, there was a few smart people in them days, just like there is now. Once there was a man—a slave, you know—on our plantation what could read and write and everything. He was a real good scholar. He would get up at two o'clock and study before he went to the field to work. You know, white folks never did like no nigger to act like he was free, and they would whip that smart nigger something awful. They kept whipping him, and finally he run away to the free states. Jones was the man what owned him; I don't remember the slave's name. He sho' was done awful, half-fed, and his folks owned right smart land, too. They was half-fed, and anytime we see that kind we would always say, "There's one of Jones's niggers."

My grandmother come over from Africa down here at Hyde's Ferry, and then they brung her on up here to Nashville. Then she was carried back to Alabama after about two years. They did talk kinda funny. They couldn't understand you, but sometime you could understand a little that they said. They would point to things that they wanted, and you would tell them what it was. She married a Indian man, and he had rings in his nose and ears. He was a slave, but they called him a Crick [Creek] Indian. He had a way of grunting when he wanted something.

Well, the free niggers was free, and then they wasn't free. They had a guardian over them. When I came to Nashville, I came up here with a lot of them kind—you know, the free ones. The guardians hire them out and got their pay, you know. Now, if you was a free nigger and did something you didn't have no business doing, you was sent to the penitentiary like anybody else. That was the difference. The slaves never went to the penitentiary for nothin' they did. They was whipped and beat on by the ole marster or the ole overseer. They didn't allow no po' white trash to light on our place; we wasn't even 'lowed to associate with them.

# My Mother Was the Smartest Black Woman in Eden

(last name unknown)

*I* began to exist in the year 1844, in a small town in Tennessee. Eden was between Nashville and Memphis and was located on a branch of the Memphis River. There were no more than four hundred people there, including the slaves. There was a post office, two stores, and a hotel in the town. The hotel was owned by Mr. Dodge, who was the uncle of my master.

I was the personal property of Mr. Jennings, who was a well-polished Southern man. He was portly in build, lively in step, and dignified in manner. Mr. Jennings was a good man. There was no disputing that. He seemed to always be in debt, and I reasoned that he was too easy, that people took advantage of his good nature. He had married a woman of the same mold, and they had three children.

I did not have the honor or dishonor of being born on a large plantation. Master Jennings had a small farm. We did not cultivate any cotton; we raised corn, oats, hay, and fruits. Most of Master Jennings' slaves were hired out. He had four families of slaves—that is, Aunt Caroline's family, Uncle Tom's family, Uncle Dave's family, and the family of which I was a member. None of these others were related by blood to us. My father had several brothers who lived on other places.

Aunt Caroline, a big mulatto woman, was very quiet and good natured. I don't remember ever hearing her fuss. Each family had a cabin, and there were but four cabins on the place. Aunt Mary, my mother's aunt, stayed with us in our cabin. She had never married or had any children.

My mother was the smartest black woman in Eden. She was as quick as a flash of lightning, and whatever she did could not be done better. She could do anything. She cooked, washed, ironed, spun, nursed, and labored in the field. She made as good a field hand as she did a cook. I have heard Master Jennings say to his wife, "Fannie has her faults, but she can outwork any nigger in the country. I'd bet my life on that."

My mother certainly had her faults as a slave. She was very different in nature from Aunt Caroline. Ma fussed, fought, and kicked all the time. I tell you, she was a demon. She said that she wouldn't be whipped, and when she fussed all Eden must have known it. She was loud and boisterous, and it seemed to me that you could hear her a mile away. Father was often the prey of her high temper. With all her ability for work, she did not make a good slave. She was too high spirited and independent. I tell you, she was a captain.

The one doctrine of my mother's teaching which was branded on my senses was that I should never let anyone abuse me. "I'll kill you, gal, if you don't stand up for yourself," she would say. "Fight, and if you can't fight, kick. If you can't kick, then bite." Ma was generally willing to work, but if she didn't feel like doing something none could make her do it. At least the Jennings couldn't make, or didn't make, her.

"Bob, I don't want no sorry nigger around me. I can't tolerate you if you ain't got no backbone." Such constant warning to my father had its effect. My mother's unrest and fear of abuse spread gradually to my father. He seemed to have been made after the timid kind. He would never fuss back at my mother, or if he did he couldn't be heard above her shouting. Pa was also a sower of all seeds. He was a yardman, houseman, plowman, gardener, blacksmith, carpenter, key smith, and anything else they chose him to be.

I was the oldest child. My mother had three other children by the time I was about six years old. It was at this age that I remember the almost daily talks of my mother on the cruelty of slavery. I would say nothing to her, but I was thinking all the time that slavery did not seem so cruel. Master and Mistress Jennings were not mean to my mother. It was she who was mean to them.

Master Jennings allowed his slaves to earn any money they could for their own use. My father had a garden of his own around his little cabin, and he also had some chickens. Mr. Dodge, who was my master's uncle and who owned the hotel in Eden, was Pa's regular customer. He would buy anything my pa brought to him, and many times he was buying his own stuff or his nephew's stuff. I have seen Pa go out at night with a big sack and come back with it full. He'd bring sweet potatoes, watermelons, chickens, and turkeys. We were fond of pig roast and sweet potatoes, and the only way to have pig roast was for Pa to go out on one of his hunting trips. Where he went, I cannot say, but he brought the booty home. The floor of our cabin was covered with planks. Pa had raised up two planks and dug a hole. This was our storehouse.

Every Sunday, Master Jennings would let Pa take the wagon to carry watermelons, cider, and ginger cookies to Spring Hill, where the Baptist church was located. The Jennings were Baptists. The white folks would buy from him as well as the free Negroes of Trenton, Tennessee. Sometimes these free Negroes would steal to our cabin at a specified time to buy a chicken or barbecue dinner. Mr. Dodge's slaves always had money and came to buy from us. Pa was allowed to keep the money he made at Spring Hill, and of course Master Jennings didn't know about the little restaurant we had in our cabin.

One day, my mother's temper ran wild. For some reason, Mistress Jennings struck her with a stick. Ma struck back, and a fight followed. Mr. Jennings was not at home, and the children became frightened and ran upstairs. For half [an] hour, they wrestled in the kitchen. Mistress, seeing that she could not get the better of Ma, ran out in the road with Ma right on her heels. In the road, my mother flew into her again. The thought seemed to race across my mother's mind to tear Mistress's clothing off her body. She suddenly began to tear Mistress Jennings' clothes off. She caught hold, pulled, ripped, and tore. Poor Mistress was nearly naked when the storekeeper got to them and pulled Ma off.

"Why, Fannie, what do you mean by that?" he asked.

"Why, I'll kill her. I'll kill her dead if she ever strikes me again."

I have never been able to find out the why of the whole thing. My mother was in a rage for two days, and when Pa asked her about it and told her that she shouldn't have done it, it was all that Aunt Caroline could do to keep her from giving him the same dose of medicine.

"No explaining necessary. You are chicken-livered, and you couldn't understand." This was all Ma would say about it.

Pa heard Mr. Jennings say that Fannie would have to be whipped, by law. He told Ma. Two mornings afterwards, two men came in at the big gate, one with a long lash in his hand. I was in the yard, and I hoped they wouldn't find me. To my surprise, I saw her running around the house, straight in the direction of the men. She must have seen them coming. I should have known that she wouldn't hide. She knew what they were coming for, and she intended to meet them halfway. She swooped upon them like a hawk on chickens. I believe they were afraid of her or thought she was crazy. One man had a long beard, which she grabbed with one hand, and the lash with the other. Her body was made strong with madness. She was a good match for them. Mr. Jennings came and pulled her away. I don't know what would have happened if he hadn't come at that moment, for one man had already pulled his gun out. Ma did not see the gun until Mr. Jennings came up. On catching sight of it, she said, "Use your gun. Use it and blow my brains out if you will."

Master sent her to the cabin, and he talked with the man for a long time. I had watched the whole scene with hands calmly clasped in front of me. I felt no urge to do anything but look on.

That evening, Mistress Jennings came down to the cabin. She stopped at the door and called my mother. Ma came out.

"Well, Fannie," she said, "I'll have to send you away. You won't be whipped, and I'm afraid you'll get killed. They have to knock you down like a beef."

"I'll go to Hell or anywhere else, but I won't be whipped," Ma answered.

"You can't take the baby, Fannie. Aunt Mary can keep it with the other children."

Mother said nothing at this.

That night, Ma and Pa sat up late, talking over things, I guess. Pa loved Ma, and I heard him say, "I'm going, too, Fannie."

About a week later, she called me and told me that she and Pa were going to leave me the next day, that they were going to Memphis. She didn't know for how long.

"But don't be abused, Puss." She always called me Puss. My right name was Cornelia.

I cannot tell in words the feelings I had at that time. My sorrow knew no bound. My very soul seemed to cry out, "Gone, gone, gone forever." I cried until my eyes looked like balls of fire. I felt for the first time in my life that I had been abused. How cruel it was to take my mother and father from me, I thought. My mother had been right. Slavery was cruel, so very cruel.

Thus, my mother and father were hired to Tennessee. The next morning, they were to leave. I saw Ma working around with the baby under her arms, as if it had been a bundle of some kind. Pa came up to the cabin with an old mare for Ma to ride and an old mule for himself. Mr. Jennings was with him.

"Fannie, leave the baby with Aunt Mary," said Mr. Jennings very quietly.

At this, Ma took the baby by its feet, a foot in each hand, and with the baby's head swinging downward she vowed to smash its brains out before she'd leave it. Tears were streaming down her face. It was seldom that Ma cried, and everyone knew that she meant every word. Ma took her baby with her.

With Ma gone, there was no excitement around the place. Aunt Mary was old and very steady in her ways. Aunt Caroline was naturally quiet, and so were all the rest. I didn't have much to do around the place, and I thought about Ma more than anyone around there knew. Yes, Ma had been right. Slavery was chuck-full of cruelty and abuse.

During this time, I decided to follow my mother's example. I intended to fight, and if I couldn't fight I'd kick, and if I couldn't kick I'd bite. The children from the big house played with my brothers, but I got out of the bunch. I stopped playing with them; I didn't care about them, so why play with them? At different times, I got into scraps with them. Everyone began to say, "Cornelia is the spit of her mother.

She is going to be just like Fannie." And I delighted in hearing this. I wanted to be like Ma now.

An uneventful year passed. I was destined to be happily surprised by the return of my mother and father. They came one day and found me sitting by the roadside in a sort of trance. I had not seen them approaching; neither was I aware of their presence until Ma spoke. Truly, I had been thinking of Ma and Pa at the time. I had dreams of seeing them again, but I thought that I would have to go to them. I could hardly believe that Ma and Pa were standing before my very eyes. I asked myself if I was still dreaming. No, I was not dreaming. They were standing over me. Ma was speaking to me.

"Puss, we've come back, me and Pa, and we've come to stay."

"Oh, Ma," I exclaimed, "I was a-praying to see you."

She and Pa embraced and caressed me for a long time. We went to the cabin, and Master Jennings was there nearly as soon as we were.

"Hello, Fannie. How did you get along?" he asked.

"Why, Mr. Jennings, you know that I know how to get along," she answered.

"Well, I'm glad to hear that, Fannie."

Ma had on new clothes and a pair of beautiful earrings. She told Aunt Mary that she stayed in Memphis one year without a whipping or a cross word.

Pa had learned to drink more liquor than ever, it seemed. At least he was able to get more of it, for there were many disagreements between Pa and Ma about his drinking. Drinkers will drink together, and Master Jennings was no exception. Pa would have the excuse that Master Jennings offered him liquor, and of course he wouldn't take it from anybody else. It was common to see them together, half-drunk, with arms locked, walking around and around the old barn. Then Pa would put his hands behind him and let out a big whoop, which could be heard all over Eden.

My temper seemed to be getting worse and worse. I was always fighting with my younger brothers and with Aunt Caroline's kids. I went around with a chip on my shoulder all the time. Mrs. Jennings had me to nurse Ellen, her youngest child, for a while, but I was mean to her, and she stopped me. I could do plenty of work in a short time, but I had such an ugly temperament. Pa would scold me about being so mean, but Ma would say, "Bob, she can't help it. It ain't her fault because she's made like that."

Our family was increased by the arrival of a baby girl. Ma was very sick, and she never did get well after that. She was cooking for Mistress Jennings one day when she came home and went to bed. She never got up. I guess Ma was sick about six months. During that time, she never hit a tap of work. She said she had brought five children in the world for the Jennings, and that was enough—that she didn't intend to work when she felt bad.

On the day my mother died, she called Pa and said, "Bob, what time is it?"

Pa went to the window and pushed it back and looked up at the sun. "It's four o'clock, Fannie."

"Well, I'm going to leave you at eight o'clock. Go tell Master Jennings to come in, and get all the slaves, too."

Pa went and returned in five minutes with old Master. "Fannie, are you any worse?" said old Master.

"No, no, Master Jennings, no worse. But I'm going to leave you at eight o'clock."

"Where are you going, Fannie?" Master Jennings asked, as if he didn't know that Ma was talking about dying.

Ma shook her head slowly and answered, "I'm going where there ain't no fighting and cussing and damning."

"Is there anything that you want me to do for you, Fannie?"

Ma told him that she reckoned there wasn't much of anything that anybody could do for her now. "But I would like for you to take Puss and hire her out among ladies, so she can be raised right. She will never be any good here, Master Jennings."

A funny look came over Master Jennings' face, and he bowed his head up and down. All the hands had come in and were standing around with him.

My mother died at just about eight o'clock.

# A Negro Has Got No Name

Mr. Reed

*F*or what intent have you come here? I don't know how many slaves my old marster had, but I know he had a yardful of niggers. I was a boy in slavery. Now, you talk about hard times, I have had hard times. I started plowing at eight years old. I called my old marster "Marster." Called the old lady "Mistress." Called Jim "Mr. Jim" and Ella "Miss Ella." That is what we learned to do. I cannot tell you all about slavery, but I can give you an outline of it. I served my old marster until Freedom taken place. My mother, my father, and five or six children was there.

I was raised on potlikker. I love it 'til today. I would take it and crumble a little bread in it. We never did get meat at night, mostly buttermilk.

I worked at herding of the cows. Every morning, I would go into the woods and drive them up. I was barefooted as a duck. Sometimes I would drive the hogs out of their warm place to warm my feet. I used to work in the tobacco patch catching worms off the leaves. Some of them worms was as big as my finger. Marster would come behind me, and if he would find a worm I would have to bite his head off. That was done in order to make me more particular and not leave worms again.

You teachers used to whip the children with a paddle or something, but my whip was a raw cowhide. I didn't see it, but I used to hear my mother tell it at the time how they would whip them with a cowhide and then put salt and pepper in your skin until it burn.

The most barbarous thing I saw with these eyes—I lay on my bed and study about it now—I had a sister, my oldest sister, she was fooling with the clock and broke it, and my old marster taken her and tied a rope around her neck—just enough to keep it from choking her—and tied her up in the backyard and whipped her I don't know how long. There stood Mother, there stood Father, and there stood all the children, and none could come to her rescue.

Now, it is a remarkable thing to tell you, some people can't see into it, but I am going to tell you, you can believe it if you want to—some colored people wouldn't be whipped by their marster. They would run away and hide in the woods, come home at night, and get something to eat, and out he would go again. Them times, they called them "runaway niggers." Some of them stayed away until after the war was over. Some of them would run to the Yankees and would bring the Yankees back and take all the corn and meat they had.

Time has been that they wouldn't let them have a meeting, but God Almighty let them have it, for they would take an old kettle and turn it up before the door with the mouth of it facing the folks, and that would hold the voices inside. All the noise would go into that kettle. They could shout and sing all they wanted to, and the noise wouldn't go outside.

Now, they had what they used to call "nigger traders," and they would call a man a "nigger buck" and a woman a "nigger wench." They would buy them and carry them down to Mississippi and put them on the cotton farms. The overseer would ride up and down the field with a gun over his shoulder to see that they kept working. When they would carry them to Mississippi, they didn't go by train, neither by automobile—there wasn't any then. They would go by foot. Someone would drive the wagon behind them, and if any of them would give out they would put them in the wagon. Many children have been taken—suckling babies sometimes—away from their mothers and carried to Mississippi.

Now, let's treasure these things up and look at them in another way. Every nationality ever before has had a better time than the Negro. Sometimes when I am on my wagon, I look at the children coming from school, and I say, "If I had had that opportunity when I was coming up, I would be 'sons of thunder.'" Then, a Negro wasn't allowed a book in his hand. What little they got, they would steal it. The white children would come out and teach them sometimes when the old folks wasn't looking.

The first Sunday school I went to was after the war. The house was an old oak tree. We used to carry our dinner and stay there from eight o'clock until four. In slavery, they used to teach the Negro that they had no soul. They said all they needed to do was to obey their mistress. One old sister was shouting in the back of the church, and her mistress was up in the front, and she looked back and said, "Shout on, old nig, there is a kitchen in Heaven for you to shout in, too."

The people used to say "dis," "dat," and "t'other." Now they say "this," "that," and "the other."

In all the books that you have studied, you never have studied Negro history, have you? You studied about the Indians and white folks. What did they tell you about the Negro? If you want Negro history, you will have to get from somebody who wore the shoe, and by and by from one to the other you will get a book.

I am going to tell you another thing. A Negro has got no name. My father was a Ransom, and he had a uncle named Hankin. If you belong to Mr. Jones and he sell you to Mr. Johnson, consequently you go by the name of your owner. Now, where you got a name? We are wearing the name of our marster.

I was first a Hale, then my father was sold, and then I was named Reed. He was brought from old Virginia someplace. I have seen my grandma and grandfather, too. My grandfather was a preacher and didn't know A from B. He could preach. I had a uncle, and he was a preacher and didn't know A from B. [I also had] a cousin who was a preacher. I am no mathematician, no biologist, neither grammarian, but when it comes to handling the Bible I knocks down verbs, breaks up prepositions, and jumps over adjectives.

To get salt to go in your bread in slavery, well, they would dig up the dirt where the fresh meat hung over and had been dripping salt, and would boil this to get the salt. They would get and parch sweet potato peelings to make coffee. You-all are blessed children; you are living on flowery beds of ease. I would to God sometimes that I was able to express myself.

Did you ever hear of Blind Tom? He could tell you how many months was in the year, how many days was in the year, and could even tell how many minutes was in a year. Blind Tom was challenged once for incorrectness in his calculations, but Tom called attention to the fact that he was figuring in a leap year.

I know plenty of [female] slaves who went with the old marster. They had to do it or get a killing. They couldn't help it. Some of them would raise large families by their owner. I know an old banker in Lebanon who gave one of his children a home after they come free.

I remember the time when Eph Grizzard was hung over the bridge. That time, they had what they called a "dummy" running from here to East Nashville. Run right down by the jail. Eph was in the jail. They had a black Mother Hubbard on him to tell him from the rest of the prisoners. They took him out of jail and went running up First Avenue to the bridge and tied the rope around his neck and threw him over. It was about three o'clock. He hung there from three until about six o'clock. They would take hold of that rope every once in a while and give it a yank. The sheriff of Goodlettsville got up on the bridge and made a speech and said, "If anybody, rich or poor, black or white, grizzly or gray, get up and say anything in this nigger's behalf, we will take them and do them the same way." Five or six man was killed trying to get to the jail to get Eph out. I was working down on the wharf at Broad this side of the Tennessee Central Station. My heart ached within me. I looked to see that bridge fall in, there was so many people on it that day. I heard that woman had a child afterwards, but I don't know. They killed him and burned him up.

Young people don't pay enough respect to old gray-headed folks. I have been a Christian ever since I was seventeen years old. I have been a minister ever since I was twenty-two. In 1885, I carried on a week's meeting in White County, had twenty-four converts and twenty additions to the church—Cumberland Presbyterian Church.

I was coming down the road one night and met a boy who was just drunk enough to have devilment in him. He came up to me and said, "Who are you?"

I said, "Reed is my name, and I'm from Hartsville, Tennessee."

He said, "What in the Hell and damnation, by God, are you doing here?"

I told him to go on about his business and that I was a preacher on my way to church.

He said, "Well, by God, you got to pray for me."

I didn't know what to do, but I stood up and looked him straight in the eye and prayed to God to deliver him. You know, you're supposed to close your eyes when you pray, but that was one time I kept mine open. I heard later that he professed religion and was a deacon in the church.

I bought this house in 1919. When I first bought it, everybody told me that I wouldn't pay for it, but by the grace of God I did. Buried my wife, daughter, and grandchild. I have been in Nashville over forty years, been a hardworking man, working and preaching. I have never been arrested in my life, never was drunk, never cussed but once—got scared and quit. Never give my parents any sass. I am out in all kinds of weather and never sick. I live close to the Lord. He will not forsake them that walk upright.

Since you ladies been talking to me so much, you got my brain stirred up to the top of my head. And if I could tell you more, I would. I can't think of everything at one time.

# We Didn't Know Nothing Else But Slavery

## Mr. and Mrs. Chapman

*Mrs. Chapman:* I was taken away from my mother when I was seven years old. That was in Hardeman County. I was brought here to Trenton by old man North. He was my guardian. I belonged to a girl, but she wasn't old enough, and she had to have a guardian for me. I was hired out to make money for that child. I lived about a mile and a half from town. I never was mistreated. They got a hundred dollars a year for me, and they had to pay my doctor's bill and feed and clothe me. I was the only slave this girl had.

After her father died, her mother married again and went to Mississippi. They said the Mississippi law allowed the husband to have the wife's property, so I was willed to this child, and the husband took my mother. That's how come we was separated. This man what willed me to this girl was named

Marshall. Colored people went in the name of their owner then. I was hired out to nurse. Some of them had slaves and some didn't. When Freedom come, I went away for a long time, and I come back and been here ever since. I went to Murfreesboro with some white folks, and they brought me back here.

When I was sick when I was little, they would make some kind of tea and put me to bed. I remember once I was hired out, and I was trying to say my alphabets backward and forward by memory. I just cried because I couldn't say them backward by memory. I don't know how I got that book, but I never did learn to say them by memory backward, but I could say them forward. I was ten years old when the war broke out.

❋

*Mr. Chapman:* I couldn't tell exactly my age. My first owner was Luke Thomas; he lived down there between Hiko and McKenzie. I stayed there until he sold me. I worked in the tobacco factory when I was a boy. I have woke up many a morning early, and old bread would be laying on the ground, and I would pick it up and eat it, and thought it was good. I have always heard that I was taken away from my mother when I was a baby, but I do remember my brother. When we was sold to Chapman, Master told him not to separate us 'cause we was brothers, and if he ever wanted to get rid of us to send us to Memphis, and he would take us back. They coulda sold me a dozen times, but they couldn't separate us, so I wasn't sold.

Me and my brother was in the trading yard before the

Civil War. We stayed in there three or four weeks. They would fix us all up and carry us in a great big old room and circle us all around every morning and every evening. They would have us up in the showroom to show us to the people. They would hit us in the breast to see if we was strong and sound. Monkeys would play with us and see if any boogies was in our heads. They would do pretty well if they found any, but if they didn't they would slap us. They had the monkeys there to keep our heads clean. They made us dance around and made us take exercise all the time we was there. They would give us molasses and bread to eat, and a little meat. We slept in little bunks that was made up 'side the wall. We didn't know nothing else but slavery—never thought of nothing else. I just know I belonged to the man who provided for me, and I had to take whatever he give me. There was some young ones and some old ones in that trading yard. They had a big time, too. Some of them had fiddles and some banjos, and they would fiddle and dance. The water that we drunk there was just as black as black could be, but it was as cold as ice.

In slavery time, they had us in quarters. There was lots of little houses all out from the big house. Luke Thomas was a pretty rough man, but all of them was good to me because they just let me have my way. I always done my work.

I was bound out since Freedom to a man name Isaac Gritholm. Bound me out when I was fifteen years old, and I was to stay 'til I was twenty-one years old. I was bound out by the Bureau [probably the Freedmen's Bureau]. All orphan children had to be bound out, so they give me my choice of two men who wanted me. I went to Isaac, but I seen I wasn't gonna learn nothing, so I quit and went on the other side of town and hired out to another fellow. Then I moved back to Trenton. I got $125 a year. Next, I hired out to a colored man named William Elder.

My master was pretty good to me, but sometimes he would whip me. I was pretty rough myself. He whipped me a heap of times, but it was mostly for fighting. One day, he whipped me for running children with snakes. He whipped me one day for fighting a white boy. The white boy had whipped me and stomped me, too, but he didn't see that. Finally, one day, that boy got after me again, and I like to killed him. He hired me out after that to old Bill Cook. I just farmed. I got along well there, too. He give me two suits of clothes, two blankets. I went home every Christmas by myself.

One time, they had a beef killed for General Forrest's regiment, but somehow or other Forrest didn't get there to eat that meat, and it begin to spoil, and they was feeding the slaves that then. I couldn't stomach it, and one day I told Marster that I had to quit work 'cause I was starving to death, and that I might as well die one way as the other. He asked me what was the matter, that the other slaves was eating all right. I told him I couldn't stand that meat, that I just couldn't stomach it. He carried me to the house and fed me from their table.

They tried to get me to tell what the colored folks was doing. They asked me if I see any of them stealing. They give me a dime, quarter, and anything to tell on them, but I told them I didn't see them stealing. I had, though, and I would eat as much as any of them of anything they had stole.

They used to have great long knives to cut the Yankees' heads off. I remember the time in the war when there was 350 "homemade Yankees." There was a lot of Southern people that fought against the South. A heap of colored people would run away to the Yankees. After they had so many, they got them up a company of soldiers. See, masters was afraid to meet their slaves after Freedom 'cause some of them was so mean they was afraid they would kill them.

One night, the Yankees was traveling all night long and was stealing everything in sight. They stole horses, and they tried to steal the mule, but every man that got up on him, the old mule would throw him. That mule throwed up to fifteen men, and not a one could stay on him. One of the soldiers said, "I'm a great mind to shoot him."

The captain said, "Don't shoot him. He freed himself."

They all said that mule sho' was a good Rebel mule. You never saw a gentler-looking mule, but he wouldn't let a one stay on his back.

One night, the niggers was going home and heard the patterollers [patrollers, white citizens who looked for slaves without written passes from their owners permitting them to be away from their farms] coming along way down the road, and they put up a grapevine all across the road, and of course they was running fast, and it throwed them every way across the road. By that time, all the niggers had run and got out of the way, and you never would know who done it. Some of them niggers was pretty smart, I tell you.

# I Got Many a Whipping

Precilla Gray

*I* think I's 107 years old. Was born in Williamson County 'fore the Civil War. Guess the reason I have lived so long was 'cause I took good care of myself and wore warm clothes and still do, wear my yarn petticoats now. Have had good health all my life. Have took very little medicine, and the worst sickness I ever had was smallpox. I's been a widow about seventy years.

My mammy died when I was young, but my daddy lived to be 103 years old. I never went to school a day in my life, married 'fore Freedom, and when I got free had to work all the time to make a living for my two chillun. One lives in California, and I lives with the other, together with my great-great-grandson, five years old, in Nashville.

My first marster and missus was Amos and Sophia Holland, and he made a will that we slaves was all to be kept among the family, and I was hired from one family to another. Was owned under the will by Haddas Holland. And then Missus Synthia married Sam Pointer, and I lived with her 'til Freedom was declared.

My first mistress had three looms, and we had to make clothes for everyone on the plantation. I was taught to weave, card, spin, and knit and to work in the fields. I was feared of the tobacco worms at first, but Aunt Frankie went along by me and show me how to pull the worms' head off. Our marster whipped us when we needed it. I got many a whipping.

Marster Amos was a great hunter and had lots of dogs, and me and my cousin had the job of cooking dog food and feeding the dogs. One day, the marster went hunting and left three dogs in the pen for us to feed. One of the dogs licked out of the pan, and we got a bunch of switches and started wearing the dogs out. We thought the marster was miles away when he walked up on us. He finished wearing the bunch of switches out on us. That was a whipping I'll never forget.

When I was hired to Missus Snythia, I worked in the fields 'til she started to raise chillun, and then I was kept in the house to see after them. Missus had a lot of cradles, and they kept two women in that room taking care of the babies and little chillun belonging to the slaves. Soon as the chillun was seven years old, they started them knitting.

Marster Sam Pointer, husband of Missus Synthia, was a good man, and he was good to us and fed and clothed us good. We wore yarn hoods, shawls, and pantalets, which was knit things that come from your shoe tops to above your knees.

The marster was also a religious man, and he let us go to church. He willed land for a colored church at Thompson Station. I belongs to the foot-washin' Baptist, called the Free Will Baptist. The marster brought my husband, William Gray, and I married him there.

When the Civil War was starting, there was soldiers in tents everywhere. I had to knit socks and helps make soldiers' coats. And during the war, the marster sent a hundred of us down in Georgia to keep the Yankees from getting us, and we camped out during the whole three years.

I remember the Ku Klux Klan. One night, a bunch of us went out. They got after us. We waded a big creek and hid in the bushes to keep them from getting us.

Ever since slavery, I've cooked for people. I cooked for Mr. Lea Dillon fifteen years. Worked at the Union Depot for years. Five years for Dr. Douglas at his infirmary. And I cooked for and raised Mrs. Grady's baby. Have worked for different folks over town to make my living. I ain't been able to work for eight years. All the ex-slaves I know have worked at different jobs like I has.

# I Was Four Years Old When I Was Put on the Block

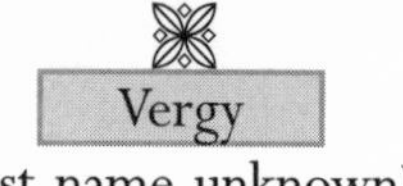


(last name unknown)

Yes, the South is a beautiful place; it's so pretty. Well, you see, honey, picking cotton wasn't so much fun to me because I was compelled. Yes, I was compelled to do it. Yes, I look around at the girls these days, and I think they ought to be mighty good and kind. They oughta be much more polite than they are; we have gone through a lot for them.

Well, I'll tell you all I can, dear. I was four years old when I was put on the block and sold. And I had to set by the cradle and rock my old mistress' baby and keep the flies off her before I was five years old. Then, of course, you know, from time to time, I had to learn how to cook and do most everything about a house. Well, dear, it was nobody but me and my brother, and we had all that to do. My mother died when I was young, way before the war. We was both together until way after the war, too.

My father belonged to another set of white people. When my mother was living, he come 'most every week to see her. Then after she died, he come every two weeks to see me and my brother. Yes'm, they both been gone on for a long time, dear, and I am surely thankful to the Lord for preserving me. I really have been well blessed, yes, indeedy, dear.

Yes, I remember when they took Pappy away from us. They said the niggers was getting ready for an uprising, and they took me and my brother way down in Cheatham County. No, I was born in Wilson County. Then my home was in Franklin, you see, but we went to Cheatham County and stayed about six months with the white folks. Course, we wasn't far away from Pappy, but, you know, far enough so he couldn't come to us, and we cried and cried. And when any of the white people went down that way, they would see Pappy, and he would send messages to us by them. Yes, dear, they would tell us exactly what Pappy said.

Then we came back. I don't know how long that was before the war broke out, but we stayed with the same white people until the war ceasted. Now, you know what happened then. They told us we were free, but of course we didn't know where to go nor nothing. The ole mistress asked me if I was glad we was free, and I, of course, childlike, say yes, I sure was, and my ole mistress sure did get mad at me. And she got mad at my brother and said she was going to send him south, just like he wasn't free and equal. Well, dear, I didn't know nothin' about what they meant, but I just knew that he was going away from me. I didn't have sense enough to know much, but I knew that much.

Well, my brother was going on a Monday morning—that was on a Saturday. So on Saturday night, I says to him, "In the morning, you take them clothes you got on now on your arm, as you come through the house, when you go to do your work." You see, I had to get breakfast, and there wasn't nobody up that time in the morning but me and my brother. I told him, "I will be in the kitchen, and you go down in the field and change your clothes and go to the courthouse and get yourself a pass." And then I told him which way to go to get to Pappy's farm. I didn't know the names nor the directions, but I just said, "You get such-and-such a road and walk 'til you get to the white fence," and like that, you know. I knew right where Pappy lived. I told him after he got to a certain place anybody would tell him where Pappy lived.

Well, on Monday morning, my old marster got up and found my brother's work wasn't finished, and I was out there cooking breakfast, and he come up and asked me, "Ain't Dave come to the house yet?"

I said, "Naw, I ain't seen him." I told that story, and I was scared, too.

Well, he looked around awhile and went on down in the yard, and then about an hour later the men come through the back going to the field across the way to do the plowing, and he asked them about Dave. None of them had seen him. Well, I was so tickled that I couldn't hardly get breakfast. And then they was talking to a man—he was a friend of me and my brother—from the next farm, and he come up in the yard, and I said, "Uncle Bob, Dave's gone."

He said, "Damn good thing," and went on through the yard. Don't nobody know about my brother but me and Uncle Bob.

Well, that was on Monday. On Tuesday, the ole boss went to town and was asking around about Dave. Well, the ole boss's sister lived right on the edge of town, and she told the ole marster that she saw him down by the courthouse early Monday morning. Well, then, by eleven o'clock, I figured he was at my father's. My pappy was sure glad to see him, and do you know, they never did know that I had something to do with that.

Well, on a Saturday, I had to churn, so I went to the well to get some water to wash the butter down from the sides of the churn. And just as I got to the well, I saw a hat through the grapevines, and somebody said, "Make haste," and I knew it was Pappy. I was the happiest child you ever heard of.

Well, I hurried and got that water and went back to the house, and I asked if Pap had been there, and ole Missus said, "No, I haven't seen him." Well, I knew he had done gone on by, down to the ole boss's father's plantation to ask his opinion about taking me to my brother. I didn't say a word; I just went on with my work.

Well, he come on back. Course, I learned all this later. He come on back and met my own bossman, and they talked and talked and talked, and after a while they both come to the house. When Pappy come in, he told me howdy, and my old marster said, "Vergy, Dave's up yonder with your pappy, and your pappy come after you. Do you want to go?"

Well, dear, I didn't know what to say, so I just hung my head and said, "I don't know."

Well, poor Pap just burst out crying. He said, "I don't want to separate you and Dave 'til you do yourself."

Well, dearie, I didn't know what to do. Pap up and told Mr. John, that was my ole boss, just how Miss Mangy, my missus, had mistreated my mother while she was living, and he told him that was why he had done a heap of things he had.

Well, Mr. John said, "Jackson, I have noticed a heap of things you have done, but I didn't know why then."

Well, finally, my ole missus owned up to it. Course, you know, dear, she kinda had to with Pappy right there. So I went on back with Pappy, after I heard how she treated Mammy.

Well, I stayed with my father, and then I married and come up here. I was up here and went into that old school what used to be right over yonder, before it was finished. My teacher was a Mr. Atchison, and then there was Miss Holly Tatler, and another white man teacher. I was in the second grade, and I married and went across to Jefferson Street one pretty moonshiny might to live with my husband. I ain't forgotten a bit of it.

I remember when my oldest daughter died. I was sitting right here sewing on a Saturday afternoon, and I saw her just as plain; she had on one of my old bonnets. Yes, my oldest daughter died, and she was sick. You see, she went to Fisk, too. She came to me over this shoulder and said to me just as plain; you see, she always had a hand for cleaning up and moving things around, and lots of times she has come and told me she was going to move this and that, and I always said it was all right with me. Well, I just jumped up and threw my sewing down, and I said, "Lord, my child ain't dead." Yes, sir, I sho' saw her just like flesh and blood.

Yes, dear, only those that gone through it know how it is to lose your child, I tell you. Every day for days and weeks, I worried something awful after she went. Lord, dear, you don't know how it worried ne. Then after that, seem like the Lord just moved away all my troubles. I felt reconciled, and something just said to me, "The Lord giveth and the Lord taketh away." Yes'm, I've lost two husbands and three children. There is nobody but me and my other daughter what lives here now.

Dear, don't you never let no white man mess with you, do you hear me? I don't want to see my color mess with them. And I tell you another thing, when the white folks steps in this house, especially the men, I demand respect. I always says, "Won't you rest your hat?" Yes, sir, just as I feel.

Just like once I was on the streetcar, and, you see, my white people that I work for had give me a book to ride on, because I had to come home every Sunday evening to see about my girls. I got on the car and handed the conductor my book, and he just looked at me kinda mean and said, "Pay your fare." I kept handing him the book; he kept saying, "Pay your fare." He let me go on by to my seat, 'cause I wasn't studying about paying my fare after I had handed him the book. He come on up to the seat I was in and said, "If you don't pay your fare, I'm going to put you off this car."

And I said, "Just put me off, put me off, and see if I don't get you put off, too." I turned round to a man what was sitting next to me and asked him, “What’s the matter with this book?” Then I asked the conductor, “What’s the matter with that book?”

And he just kept saying, “Pay your fare.”

Then some poor old colored man said, “Here, lady. Here’s a nickel for your fare.” You see, he was scared, ’fraid the man would put me off. But I wasn’t.

Well, I come on home, and when I got back, if I didn’t tell them white people, honey—I sure told them all about it. And I asked them, “What you got written on that book, ‘nigger’ or something?” And they sure had that conductor put off.

# I Expect I Am the Oldest Man in Nashville

I'm about played out now. Yes, I like to look at the ladies sometimes. I don't get out much now. Last night was a cold night, wasn't it?

I expect I am the oldest man in Nashville. Nearest we can come to making out my age, I am 'bout 120 years old. I don't know it exactly 'cause when the war broke out they lost the Bible [slaves' birth dates were customarily recorded in the Bible of their white family].

I was a young man when the stars fell, and you know that was a long time ago [1833]. I seen them; they just fell and went out before they hit the ground. How come me to see it? We had just killed hogs and had the meat hanging up on poles, and I had to watch it all night. I had a fire out there, you know. It scared a lot of them, but it didn't do no good. Somebody started blowing the horn what you call the dogs with, and they started hollering that Gabriel was blowing his trumpet. I never was a kind of man to worry about any one thing.

I was born right over yonder where Purdy had his school, right over there back of Jubilee Hall. It was woods around here then. My marster's oldest son was my father. My marster never was very mean to me. He knocked me around once. I was driving the calves home, and I tied a can around their necks and made them holler. He whipped me about that. My mother cooked, washed, and do things like that around the house. Mistress used to ask me what that was I had on my head, and I would tell her [it was] hair, and she said, "No, that ain't hair, that's wool." They wasn't mean to none of the slaves. He didn't have but 'bout ten or fifteen slaves. They lived in different little cabins around the yard. He didn't have no overseers.

I didn't do much when I was a boy, just played around all the time and pull a little grass out of the pavement. I had a easy time compared to some. Mother didn't have a husband 'til after the war. She stayed right in the house with the white folks. My wife had good folks, too.

I was out to Fort Negley, and they come and carried me to jail, and I stayed there eight weeks—that's how come I didn't have to go to war. [His owners contrived this means of preventing his running away to the Yankees.] My mother come there and brought me some clothes and something to eat, and the next day they come and carried me home. My mother didn't know where I was at first. I looked like a skallin [skeleton] when I first come out, I was so poor. I was weak and half-starved, too. Then it woulda took me from now 'til night to walk to Jubilee Hall.

I don't like slavery nohow. They believe in tramping you like a dog. They used to take a child out and sling it up against a tree and sling its brains out. I never did see that, but my uncle coming from Virginia saw it. They used to stand slaves backwards to the river and shoot them off in the river [during the Civil War]. Just meanness, that's all. They did every kind of thing. They used to stand slaves up on a platform down on the public square and sell them like they was dogs or horses. It was awful.

We used to raise oats, corn, and things like that. Get up at daybreak, went out to feed the stock, and come in, eat breakfast, and then out to the field. We used to have hog jowl, cabbage, potatoes, and different things like that to eat. Sometimes we would have it for breakfast and dinner, too.

Mother worked for them a good while after the war. I didn't have sense enough to feel any way about it. All I cared about was fiddling and dancing. It was "come day, go day, God send Sunday" with me.

In the summertime, we would go around half-naked. We didn't wear nothing but one piece, a shirt that come down below your knees.

After Freedom, I used to go hunting a whole lot. Sometimes I would kill fifty rabbits. I wore them long boots, and sometimes I would be barefooted.

I waited on my marster 'til he died. He took sick in Arkansas. He inhaled the scent of his brother who was dead, and he took sick and died. After my old marster died, old

Mistress give me an acre of ground for waiting on her. That was after Freedom.

A man killed his brother. They tried to 'press him in the Rebel army. He told them he wouldn't go and leave his wife and chillun, and they shot him down. It was awful to try to make a man leave his wife and family to go to the army. It's awful to think of slavery anyhow.

I pretended to profess religion one time. I don't hardly know what to think about religion. They say God killed the just and unjust; I don't understand that part of it. It looks hard to think that if you ain't done nothing in the world, you be punished just like the wicked. Plenty folks went crazy trying to get that thing straightened out.

They used to have corn shuckings and dances all night. It was generally on Saturday night. Oh, no, you couldn't think of going to the white folks' church. Niggers had their own churches, and white folks had theirs.

I done wore myself out now; I ain't no-'count for nothing. I used to work up to Fisk until a few years ago. I did all the carpentry work up there. The last job I worked on was the new publishing house downtown.

There was some free Negroes. Nobody bothered them if they had some white man to stand for them. Some of them was carpenters, dig cisterns, and things like that. They would go from one place to another working sometimes.

I was riding on a streetcar long after Freedom, and I passed the cemetery where my father was buried. I started cussing: "Let me get off this damn car and go see where my goddamn father is buried, so I can spit on his grave." I got no mercy on nobody who bring up their children like dogs. How could any father treat their child like that? Bring them up to be ignorant like they did us. If I had my way with them, all I would like to have is a chopping block and chop every one of their heads off. Of course, I don't hate them; that is good. There are some good white folks. Mighty few, though. Old General Jackson said before he would see niggers free he would build a house nine miles long and put them in it and burn every one of them up. A dirty old rascal—now he is dead and gone.

They lynched Eph Grizzard about a white woman. I used to go around some myself, but I ain't going to say much about that. I've done a little of everything, I can tell you that.

# I Never Worries No Matter What Happens

Patsy Hyde

Don't know how old I is. I was born in slavery and belonged to the Brown family. My missus was Jean R. Brown, and she was kin to Abraham Lincoln, and I used to hear them talking 'bout living in a log cabin. When Lincoln died, she had her house draped in black. Marster Brown was also good to his slaves. The missus promise Marster Brown on his deathbed never to let us be whipped, and she kept her word. Some of the overseers on other plantations would tie the slaves to a stake and give them a good whipping for something they ought not to done.

All colored people wore cotton goods, and the younger boys run round in their shirttails. My missus knit all the white chillun's stockings, and she made me some. I had to hold the yarn on my hands when she was knitting. I remembers one time I was keeping flies off the table using a bunch of peacock feathers, and I went to sleep, and she told me to go back to the kitchen. I went and finish my nap.

One day, ole Uncle Elick woke Marster Brown from his afternoon nap, telling him that the prettiest men that I ever seed was passing by on the road. He went to the window and said, "Good God, it's them damn Yankees." My white folks had a pretty yard and garden. Soldiers come and camped there. I'd slip to the window and listen to them. When they was fighting at Fort Negley, the cannons would jar our house. The soldiers' band played on Capitol Hill [in Nashville] and play "Rally Round the Flag, Boys, Rally Round the Flag."

The slaves would take their old iron cooking pots and turn them upside down on the ground near their cabins to keep the white folks from hearing what they was saying. They claimed that it showed that God was with them.

In slavery time, peoples believed in dreams. I remembers one night I dreamed that a big white thing was on the gatepost without a head. I told my mammy, and she said God was warning us.

I don't remember much 'bout the Ku Klux Klan, but I does remember seeing them parade one time in Nashville. [This was probably in 1869, immediately preceding the disbandment of the Klan at Fort Negley.]

I remember the first streetlights in Nashville. When the lamp man would come round and light the lamps, they would yell out, "All is well!" And I also remembers the Southern money going out and Yankee money coming in, and also when there wasn't any coal here, and everything was wood, and most of this town was in the woods.

The slaves was told they would get forty acres of ground and a mule when they was freed, but they never got it. When we was free, we was turned out without a thing. My grandmammy was an ole mammy [a nursemaid], and the missus kept her. After Freedom, a lot of Yankee nigger gals come down here and hire out.

When I was a young girl, hundreds of people went to the wharf at the foot of Broadway on the first Sunday in May of every year for the annual baptizing of new members into the Baptist churches of the city. Thousands of white people would crowd both sides of the Cumberland River, Broadway, and the Sparkman Street bridge to witness the doin's. On leaving the churches, the pastor would lead the parade to the river, and some of the members would be overcome with religious feelings, and they would hop up and down, singing and shouting all the time, or maybe they would start to running down the street, and the brethren would have to run them down and bring them back.

We used to have them camp meetings, and they was honeys, and I enjoy them, too. We wore bandanna handkerchiefs on our heads and long shawls over our shoulders. At these meetings, they had all kind of good things to eat and drink.

After my Freedom, I done washing and ironing for white families. Never married, but I never worries no matter what happens, and that's maybe because of my living so long.

Things today is mighty bad. Not like the ole days. World is going to end soon.

After I got too feeble to do washing and ironing for my living, I went to the Relief Office to get them to helps me, but they wouldn't do a thing. I had no place to go or no money to do with. This colored woman took me in and does all she can for me, but now she is disable to work, and I don't know what to do. If'n I could get a small grocer order each week 'til I get the old age pension, it would help lots.

# My Father and Abe Lincoln Was First Cousins

*I* am eighty-eight years old, born March 15, 1843. I am a preacher and a tinner. I preached fifty-six years. I am on a pension now.

I was sold four times in my life. First time by my half-brother. He carried me away from Springfield when I was seven years old, and when I had come to the age of twelve my half-brother sold me. I was mighty near like Joseph, and my own half-brother sold me. His father and my father and Abe Lincoln was first cousins. My father was a Mudd. Abe Lincoln and him was brother and sister's children. My brother was on the colored side. [He] carried me to see the old folks. And when I was there, I saw a picture on the wall, and I said, "That picture looks mighty like Abe Lincoln." And the old woman there looked like she had worn out six or seven bodies with the same face, and said that it ought to, because it was Abe Mudd, and they were first cousins.

The second time, I was sold to Woods in Osceola. Third time, I was sold to Dr. Whitson in Osceola. Dr. Whitson bought ten of us in that drove and brought us from Osceola to Tullahoma, Tennessee, in 1860, prior to the beginning of the Civil War. Dr. Whitson started with those ten to Mississippi to sell when he got to Stevenson, Alabama. He met Ben Harris coming from his farm in Mississippi. Harris met Dr. Whitson, and Harris bought all ten of us and brought us back to Nashville and my finish of slavery.

I was partially reared out here on Fourth Avenue. It was known as Nolensville, and I stayed there until 1864. In '65, I run away and come to the Yankees. I come here during the Civil War, worked for the government one month.

It is very seldom you can get a colored person to tell you anything about slavery. The white folks ain't gonna tell you. Women wasn't anything but cattle. We find that the suffering from slavery was plenty bad. Some of us had good owners, and some of us had bad. The meanest of all my owners was the last one. Of course, I cannot complain much. I was only a boy, but I knew enough to understand the pressure of slavery and what the colored went through.

The white folks would not give us no butter and things like that, and I would go over to the springhouse to get it, and I would sometimes bring as much as two pounds of butter in my bosom. I would always have something hid in the springhouse, and I would prize the log on the springhouse open, and when the white folks would come down to the springhouse to get butter and stuff, they would be taken out, and we would have gotten it and given it to the runaway Negroes. I killed chickens and stuck them in my bosom. I have toted eggs in my bosom. Aunt Letty would make our breeches with short pockets in them, and I would get her to make my pockets large, and I would fill them with strings, and up in the storeroom I would tote sugar and flour and take them to Aunt Letty. I bet I have toted about twenty gallons of blackberry jelly in my pockets to Aunt Letty. I would kill a hen and stick it in my bosom, and she would cook it. We had a big apple orchard. We could have thirty or forty barrels of apples, and I would tote apples out through the henhouse and get out like the hens come in. If I would want to get out, I would look out to see if no one was coming. And if no one was coming, I would push them around to the front and let them drop out, and I would come out after.

Yes, we had bacon and cabbages, and they would issue it out. The cook would be at the white [plantation] house. She had a window, and she would call the boy when dinner was ready. Then we would come up and get it in pans. We had the fattest meat and thick bread. I was the churner, and sometimes I would churn twelve times on Monday. They would take the butter off the milk, and sometimes I would take the churn and pour the milk to the hogs.

When I came to Nashville, it was nothing but cane and thickets, but all that was cut out at the time of the war. Course, during the war, there was so much killing. Right over there on Seventh Avenue, there was one of the finest springs the city ever known. Where there was hydrant water, you could see five hundred wagons getting water, and you could see wagons going round peddling water. All this what you see now, it was nothing but brambles. I know it just like it was yesterday.

Yes, right down here was where I was brought in 1856 from Osceola. I was in the sale house right where the Morris Memorial Building is. Going toward the square, a little store was built of white bricks. Well, that was the sale house, before that was torn down. Right where the YMCA is, there was two sale houses, right down on Cedar. And was another sale house. Made four right on the square, right in front of Market Square. There was a sale block where they carried the Negroes and auctioned them off. Where the auction block was, the A.M.E. Sunday school bought that. They are out on Eighth and Lea Avenue, but that was where the African Methodist organized their Sunday school, right there in that building. And when they got so large they couldn't manage it, they bought that place on the corner out there. And right where that old building is now, those Irishmen got rich selling Negroes to white folks, and whiskey and beer.

Now, I know when every Negro school was organized. The first school for colored was McKeeve's School. I went to McKeeve's School, and I was promoted every Monday morning. I used to couldn't come to school but about twice or three times a month, and the teacher wanted to know how I would know so much and be away nearly all the time. I was working for Mr. Moore then. Do you know where Dr. Roman lives? The first school was on that ground. Dr. McKeeve followed the army, and then after the war he founded the school. At the close of the war, General Fisk bought the barracks where the colored library is. If you notice back of the building, you will see some frame buildings that was barracks after the war. Where the library is built, that is where the school was. That's why I call that "old Fisk University."

Dr. White organized the Fisk Jubilee Singers [during the] time I was at McKeeve's School. I went to school for three weeks, and in the day I was working with Mr. Moore. They organized the Jubilee Singers, and I was in the first crowd. Dr. White took a good deal of pains with me 'cause I had such a good voice. The first five hundred dollars that was paid in the building of Jubilee Hall, we made it singing round town and places, and we paid it in that. After that, Mr. Moore said they thought it would be best for me to learn the trade, 'cause I would break down in the singing troupe and would not have any trade. Dr. White didn't want to give me up, but I thought it was better after I was a motherless boy that I get a trade, so I took up the trade.

Right where the Jubilee Hall stands was Fort Gillam. You remember, on the campus front of Jubilee was an old rock. That is why those stones are there. The faculty ought to have those stones painted and labeled. They tore down those stones when they went to build Jubilee Hall.

Roger Williams [another school] was organized right down on Hampton Street between Twelfth and Eleventh in a big government building. When they got too numerous for that building, they moved to another building where there is now a big farm, and they repaired that old building, and that put the school there. They bought a place on Hillsboro Pike right opposite of Vanderbilt and built a large building there. It got burned down for some reason, and the white folks would not let them build it back, and they had to go out where they are now.

And right where Vanderbilt is, old Mrs. Taylor, she owned a farm, and they built the Vanderbilt building right on her place.

When I came to Nashville in 1856, the capitol wasn't finished then. The walls of the capitol have been finished since the Civil War. And those walls were all quarried on Pearl Street and Jo Johnston; that was a fine quarry.

I have been superannuated. I am a natural grammarian. I love botany and zoology, too. I spent eight years in Central Tennessee School, studying for the ministry. In 1884, I was examined for deaconship. In 1889, I was elected as teacher in the Tennessee Teachers College, to teach electricity.

In 1890, I found my mother. And I was gone from her thirty-three years before I knew anything about her. I wrote letters of inquiry until I found about her. She was no further than Springfield, Kentucky. I went to get her, and she wanted to come, but she belonged to the Catholic Church, and they wouldn't let me have her. She was seventy-three years old then, and earning wages. They drove me out of there when they found I was a Protestant. It soon spread all over Springfield about what I said and what I did—that I come after my mother, and I was a Protestant, and she was a Catholic, and she belonged to them. And I never saw my mother again. She died about two years after.

Then I came back home and taught at the technical school, at tinning and carpentering. At the same time, I groveled with English and struggled with a little science along with that. I learned tinning directly after I came from the

Government Service Guarantee. You have heard of Reverend Moore from Fisk University? His father was a tinner from the old school, and when he came out he wanted to learn the trade, and he went to his father and took me with him. I was a grown man then and arranged myself to learn the trade. I worked at Central Training College. Taught there eight years, and in that eight years I issued five diplomas.

I was here when there was no streetcars. The first cars was horsecars. The colored rode with them, but it wasn't long before they changed and got it. Yes, Negro men and their whiskey. They didn't treat their own women right, and they wouldn't treat the white women right, and they got so bad that Negroes couldn't ride on the railroad, but they saw that they were losing money, and they put a partition in the horsecar, just like the railroad. At first on the horsecars, they put the Negroes in the front, but that didn't suit them, and they put the Negroes in the back. I used to tell them when I was traveling on the train, "Well, we Negroes are treated royal, all right. You put us right in front, and the white folks ride in the back, so that they can smell the Negroes." Then they started to put the partition on the railroad.

# They Were Saving Me for a Breeding Woman

Name unknown

My mother was born in Mississippi and brought here. My father was born in Maryland. He was an old man when he come here, but they just bought them and put them together. My mother was young—just fifteen or sixteen years old. She had fourteen children, and you know that meant lots of wealth. Yes, it was a large family of us, but there's just two of us living now. I have a half-sister in Washington. I had just two children to live, a boy and a girl, and they both died after they got grown.

Just the other day, we were talking about white people when they had slaves. You know, when a man would marry, his father would give him a woman for a cook, and she would have children right in the house by him, and his wife would have children, too. Sometimes the cook's children favored him so much that the wife would be mean to them and make him sell them. If they had nice long hair, she would cut it off and wouldn't let them wear it long like the white children. They would buy a fine girl and then a fine man and just put them together like cattle; they would not stop to marry them. If she was a good breeder, they was proud of her.

I was stout, and they were saving me for a breeding woman, but by the time I was big enough I was free. I had an aunt in Mississippi, and she had about twenty children by her marster. On Sunday, they would get us ready to go to church. They would dress us up after we ask them if we could go, and they would have me walk off from them, and they would look at me, and I'd hear them saying, "She's got a fine shape; she'll make a good breeder." But I didn't know what they were talking about.

There was another man in Nashville, on the Granny White Pike, and he had a regular farm of slaves; he'd just raise them to sell. He had a sugar plantation in Louisiana, and he would sell some and send some down there, and then he would hire some out around here. He would let all that was near enough come home for Christmas, but on New Year's Day you would see a string of them as long as from here to Fisk going south. They would have two covered wagons to carry the children and some of the women in, but the others would be walking. One of the wagons would be in front and the other behind the walkers.

We children didn't know the grief of it then, but they would sell them apart. Of course, some of the buyers would have pity on them and buy them all that was in one family, if possible. Old Gale [the speaker's master] was mighty nice about that. He had a woman once, and he caught her crying several times and asked her to tell him what the trouble was. So finally, she told him that they sold her children away from her and didn't give her a chance to tell them good-bye. She said she didn't mind being sold, but they took her to town, and she didn't know they were going to sell her, and she didn't get to tell her children she was gone. Old Gale saw the man and got him to let the children come to see her one Christmas, and he would let her go to see them the next.

Then there was old Sam Watkins. He would ship the husbands out of bed and get in with their wives. One man said he stood it as long as he could. One morning, he just stood outside, and when Watkins got with his wife he just choked him to death. He said he knew it was death, but it was death anyhow, so he just killed him. They hanged him. There has always been a law in Tennessee that if a Negro kill a white man it means death.

Now, mind you, all of the colored women didn't have to have white men. Some did it because they wanted to, and some were forced. They had a horror of going to Mississippi, and they would do anything to keep from it. A white woman would have a maid sometimes who was nice looking, and she would keep her, and her son would have children by her. Of course, the mixed blood, you couldn't expect much from them.

The meanest thing they did was selling babies from the mother's breast, but all of them didn't do that. The man across the street and our folks seemed a little more enlightened. It just seemed that some of them would buy a woman with children just to sell her away. They would tell her to take the market wagon to town, and when she got there they could sell her, and she wouldn't know what he was taking her for 'til he started selling her.

There was an old man lived on the Shelby place, Dr. Shelby. And somebody was always suing him for beating people almost to death and then selling them. They would die two or three days afterwards. His slaves never saw their house in the daytime. They would go to work at night and come back at night.

Dr. Gale had about twenty-five of us slaves up here in Tennessee, but I reckon he had thousands in Mississippi, and lots of them was his children. They had to work just like we did, and they had to call him "Marster," too, and the overseer would take them down and whip them just like the others. The mother would have a better time, but the children didn't. The only advantage they had was that Marster Gale wouldn't sell them. My grandfather was an Irishman, and he was a foreman, but he had to whip his children and grandchildren just like the others.

I reckon I was eight or nine years old when the war came—might have been older than that because I can remember too much to have been so young. I remember when the white people were getting up a regiment and drilling round, and they would give them farewell parties. I remember the Civil War better than I remember the World War. We were right between the two armies when Hood's raid was. And when all the fighting was, we was right between the two battlefields. They started fighting on Wednesday, and they fought until Friday, and then the Rebels throwed down their arms and give up. The women just throwed up their hands and hollered, "Nasty, stinking cows! Just running! Why don't they fight?"

We were called "Dr. Gale's free niggers." He never did allow the patterollers on our place. My old marster had some relatives here named McNairy, and he always looked after it if they bothered us. We had to get a pass to go off the place, but McNairy's place was right joining ours, and right across the road was Mrs. Cantrell's place, and we could go to their places without a pass.

Some of the others [owners] would shut down on them [slaves]. Many a time, they'd have church there, and there was a thicket near, and the patterollers would go in there and wait and whip them as they were leaving church. Old Alfred Williams was the preacher, and he would send somebody after his marster Andrew, and he would sit there with his gun on his lap to keep them from whipping him 'til his marster would come and take him home. Yes, he was colored, and a slave, too, but they used to have good meetings there 'til old Mr. Cantrell said they would have to stop that. He was a Presbyterian minister, and he said they had God troubled on the throne.

And they didn't 'low no two or three men to be standing about talking either. They feared they was talking about being free. They didn't bother the women that way, but no man better not try it. They would search the slave houses for books, too.

During the war, the colored men that had wives at other

places, they wouldn't let them go to visit them at all. They said they'd get to talking, and they threatened to shoot any who tried to go.

I remember when they nominated Abe Lincoln and Jeff Davis just as well as I remember when they nominated Hoover and Roosevelt. We children heard the old folks talking about it. Yes, I'll tell you. They would go round to the windows and listen to what the white folks would say when they was reading their papers and talking after supper. Sometimes they would be laughing and talking in their marster's house while the argument was going on between the two sides, and the marsters would say, "You needn't be laughing and talking. You ain't gonna be free." Now, the slaves wouldn't be talking about being free at all, but they might just feel a little jolly, and the marsters would say that to them.

My mother hired me out during the war, and I learned how to use a knife and fork by looking at the folks there. My folks were away during most of the war. In September, they would always go south because it was warmer, and they went like this in the fall, and in the spring the Battle of Fort Donelson came off, and the Yankees took Nashville, so they were cut off. Our young mistress was sick, and they left her here. The day they took Fort Donelson, the soldiers had a dress parade, and a newsboy was running round with papers, hollering, "Extra! Extra! Fort Donelson has fallen, and the enemy will be here tomorrow!" I remember young Mistress took some table linen and started south to her folks. We could hear the Rebels singing as they retreated, "I wish I was in Dixie." And right now at the reunions when those old soldiers start singing that, they just jump around and shout.

And the Yankees were singing as they advanced,

> "It must be now the kingdom coming,
> In the year of Jubilee;
> Old Marster run away
> And the darkies stay at home."

Yes, the slaves stayed and took care of the place 'til the white folks came back, and some of them stayed there 'til they died. Colonel took charge of the place when our folks were away, but he had to go to war. He had been in West Point, and he said that before he'd let his mother bake bread and his sister wash and iron, he would wade in blood up to his stirrups. And he went off to war, and he got blown to pieces in one of the first battles he fought in.

Oh, they tried to scare us, said the Yankees had horns, but when we saw them with their blue clothes, brass spurs on their feet, and their guns just shining, they just looked pretty to us.

None of our slaves went to war. They were all either too old or too young on our plantation. Some might have went from the Mississippi plantation.

You notice most white people in the South say "Daddy" and "Mother." In slavery time, colored couldn't say "Papa"; they had to say "Daddy" and "Mammy." And when they got free, they started saying "Papa," and then the white people started saying "Daddy." Now the colored are right back at "Daddy" again; they will copy after them.

# I Have No Kin in This World

Dan Thomas

*I* was born in slavery in 1847 at Memphis, Tennessee, and my marster was Deacon Allays. My mammy was the cook at the big house. My mammy died soon after I was born, and the missus raised me on a bottle. Marster and Missus treat us—all the slaves—kindly, and plenty to eat, and everyone was happy. I don't know nothing 'bout my daddy or where he went. I have no kin in this world. All I ever heard was that all my folks come from Africa. My missus would tell us that I must be good and mind, and everybody will like you, and if she died they would take care of me. That is what they have done.

I seed them sell a lot of slaves in Mississippi, just like horses and hogs, one time when the marster and mistress made a trip down there. Lots of times, they made trips round the country, and they always took me along. I seed some cruel marsters that hitched up their slaves to plows and made them plow like horses and mules did.

After the slaves got their freedom, they had to look after themselves, so they would work on the plantation 'til they got so they could rent a place, like you rent houses and farms today. Some got places where they worked for wages.

I worked round the house 'til I was about ten years old, and the marster put me to work in his big whiskey business. When I got about twenty-one years old, I would go out to collect bills from Marster's customers, and it took me 'bout a week to get all round. I wasn't 'lowed to take money but had to get their checks. I also worked eighteen years as a bartender. Marster and Missus died 'bout four years 'fore whiskey went out of the United States. I stayed with them 'til they died.

After Marster and Missus dies, the doctor says I would have to leave Memphis on account of my health. I come to Nashville and got a job at the powder plant during the World War, and stayed there 'til it was over. I then gets work at Foster and Creighton in Nashville 'til they told me that I was too old to work. I makes my living now by hauling slop and picking up things that the white folks throw in their trash pile, and some of it I sell to the paper and junk dealers. The white people help me now also.

I voted three times in my life, but that was a long time ago. I voted for Teddy Roosevelt and Woodrow Wilson, and my last vote was 'bout two years ago.

# I Was Sharp As a Tack

Lucy

(last name unknown)

*I* was a slave a good many years before the Civil War. The war broke out when I was in Bowersville, Texas. Master was a good man. I had a young mistress, and she was from Hampton, Virginia. Her father give me to her for a wedding present when she married, you know. I was supposed to be a kinda maid and companion for her. I was a very delicate child and of course wasn't much use on a big plantation, so he was kinda glad to get rid of me. In that way, you see, I got to do a lot of traveling.

My old master was named Mr. Gillum. I never called him "Marster" or nothing. When the war broke out, I was sent to Key West, Florida, me and my old missus. You see, her husband was the property of the United States—standing army, you know—and of course they moved from place to place. Then, after we went to Key West, we went to New York, then back to Louisville, and after that time our headquarters was Philadelphia. About two weeks after he come from Key West, he was ordered here to Nashville to take charge and be quartermaster. Now, during the Battle of Nashville, he was in Knoxville. Yes'm, I did get to travel round right smart for a nigger in them days. My mistress and master was nice to me, too.

I sho' 'nough was sassy. I didn't pick nobody to sass neither. I sassed everybody. Mr. Gillum was offered a thousand dollars for me when I was fourteen years old, 'cause I sassed a nigger trader. Yes, I sho' sassed him. He shook his fist in my face, and I just sassed him something awful. Then he started after me, and I kept looking back and kinda running, and I yelled, "Gillum will kill you if you touch me!" He come up to me and asked where I lived, and he told me to get there quick. I sho' told him where I lived and just flew home.

Well, that old nigger trader come on down to the house, and I went to the door and let him in and went and told Mr. Gillum there was a man to see him. I didn't say "gentleman," I just said "man."

Then they went to talking, and I peeked through the keyhole and listened, too, and Mr. Gillum say, "Why, her weight in gold can't buy her, that's all." Yes, my white folks was good to me.

Well, it was a long time before I knew that I was a slave, you know. And then one day, ole Miss Gillum say to me, "Lucy, I am going to set you free." Well, I began to understand things then, and now I know that the Lord just opened the way for the po' nigger. Don't you believe that? You see, the reason I didn't hardly know that I was supposed to be a slave was 'cause I was really ole Miss' housekeeper—kept house, took care of her money, and everything. She was one of these kinda women that couldn't keep up with nothing, kinda helpless, you know, and I just handled her money like it was mine almost.

Now, in them days, we had to travel in boats. I remember once when we was traveling on the boats we met a boatful of slaves going down south to be sold. I jest thought it was terrible then, although I was a little tyke. Yes, we was traveling, and we come to a farm one Sunday and decided to rest and wash up for the rest of our journey. Now, I and ole Miss Gillum, too, far as that goes, had been raised in a Christian home, and, chile, when we saw them slaves working out in the fields and around on the plantation just like it was Monday or any other weekday, well, me and ole Missus was just shocked, and we thought it was something scandalous. You see, I was young, and I didn't know and understand conditions as they was then, like I can see things now. I remember I says to ole Missy, "Lawd, they wouldn't work me like that, just like it was Monday morning. No, sirree." Oh, chile, I was one sassy chile!

She said, "But Lucy, they have to work if they wants them to."

And me, I was just young and smart, you know. I says, "Well, I sho' wouldn't work on Sunday for nobody." Now wasn't that silly? You see, I didn't know, that was all.

Well, then we was on our way to Texas. We stayed at Galveston all night, I remember, and we was coming on toward San Antonio that next morning, and we saw a large white house, and we stopped there, and, chile, there sho' was a mean ole woman stayed there. Why, she just worked her poor ole nigger slaves something awful. She worked 'em until way in the night. I don't believe they got any sleep. Honey, that sho' was a mean ole woman there.

I remember when I went to bed that night, the ole woman slave—the cook, you know—was piddling round in the kitchen, and that ole woman was just actually driving her. Well, that ole woman had a parrot, one of these ole talking kind, and he was smart and talkative like me. The next morning, the po' ole slave come out and say breakfast was ready; it was before six o'clock then. Then the crazy ole parrot say right loud, "Listen at that damn nigger talking about breakfast ready, and the coffee ain't even made."

Well, I turned round and spoke that parrot out. I say, "Shut yo' mouth, drat you," and I said a whole lots more, too. And that ole white woman heard me, and she went in and told Mrs. Gillum.

Well, you know, course ole Missy didn't get after me or nothin', but she told me after a while, "Lucy, don't you say nothin' to that woman. You will make her whip that poor ole slave. She is terrible mean."

I was awful airish and smart, you know, and I laughs and says, "Huh, if she tried to whip me, I would hit her back."

Ole Missy, she just smile and say, "Oh, Lucy, you really just don't know."

So you see now that I really didn't know. Ole Missy told Mr. Gillum about what I said to that ole parrot, when she thought I wasn't listening, and he just laughed fit to kill hisself. I was one sassy chile.

Yes, honey, sometimes I get to thinking about it now. I remember my ole missy used to have a little red flannel bag, had paint on it like they have nowadays—rouge, you know. And she used to rub with that little flannel and make her cheeks real nice and rosy. And course me, smart, would go right behind her and rub my cheeks, too, and course I wasn't the right color. I would say, "My cheeks don't get red as your'n."

And she would say, "Lucy, you have to rub 'em harder."

I didn't know, I was so silly and young, but smart. Chile, I was sharp as a tack.

My ole master owned over one hundred head of slaves, and he didn't 'low nobody—I mean nobody—to hit one of his niggers. He didn't even 'low us to let white chillun hit us without hitting 'em back. We was always called "Jones' free niggers." Yes, but I was born in Virginia.

Why, one time, I had seven chillun in school. Three of 'em lives right here in Nashville; the other one is married and lives in Hot Springs; but the rest is dead. I am a mother of fourteen chillun. No'm, you sho' would never believe it by looking at me, would you? Two of 'em went to Fisk.

I went back there about twenty years ago, and all the folks what lived round there and knowed my sister and me was sho' nice to me. I stayed almost six weeks. All the white folks was so nice to me. Course, all my own old white people was dead 'cept just one family. He is a lawyer. His name was Howard. Me and him used to fuss and fight something awful when we was kids. When I went back there, he said, "Lucy, I remember Grandpa give me a good beating about you, didn't he?" I hadn't forgot it either, and we laughed about it a lot.

Well, they used to say a bird comes in the house, it sho' going to be death right there in the family. Why, a bird come in this here house and flew right on my daughter's shoulder before she died. She was sixteen years old. I was so nervous from it. The bird had been eating pokeberries, and he left some on her dress. Well, she went on to church, and coming back she fell down, and she come on home to me just about half-crying, you know. She always in poor health. She come on home and went to school Monday, Tuesday, and Wednesday, and I had just went to see a lady about giving her fancy-work lessons. Well, she went to school on Wednesday morning, and in a little while Martha come in. Martha was the youngest. I said, "Where is Lucy?" And then somebody come and told me my child had done got sick at school, and I said, "Lord, don't let my child die in school, please." I told Mr. King to go get a horse and buggy and go get her, and he was so nervous he couldn't hardly go, and so I sent for Dr. Hadley and Reverend Taylor, and they had done sent her home in a carriage. They didn't tell me for a long time that she done had a real heavy hemorrhage at school. She lived just three weeks, right to a day, poor child. And she was the only one named for me; her pa named her for me. And everybody said she looked like me, too. She had the prettiest hair. When she died, she had a sick spell and was gone just that quick.

If I live to see the twenty-seventh day of next month, I will be seventy-nine years old. I professed religion in 1866, and the Lord have taken good care of me, I think. The only real sin I committed, I was a dancer, that's all.

Yes, I was here in Nashville when they killed Grizzard. I remember those white people. They brought him and hung him over the bridge. The white people oughta been stoned to death for a trick like that. They brought that poor nigger up here from down in Tennessee. Well, after it happened, the people said the girl's father give that old white girl to that man hisself. I remember there was a girl working at the hotel soon after that by the same name, and them old white folks and the steward asked her if she was any relation to them, and she said yes, she was a sister, and they fired her at the hotel. Yes, sirree, they got rid of her right away. And that was the most disgraceful thing what ever happened in Nashville, and I tell you the real sho'-'nough white folks was sick of it.

# There Wasn't No Learning Going On in Slavery

Name unknown

*I* don't know exactly how old I am, but I recollect far enough back to remember the war. Niggers couldn't have no books then. There wasn't but two colored people there who could read and write—one woman and one man. After Freedom, preachers would want to know how to read the Bible, and the others wanted to learn, too, and this woman who could read told them they would have to learn how to spell first, and she told them what they would have to do. So they got about two dozen of these old-fashion spelling books. She carried them to Bluff Springs and taught them their ABC's. It was two years after Freedom before we had any teachers. There wasn't no learning going on in slavery, I can tell you. They wasn't 'lowed to touch a book. If you did, you got a good whipping.

The colored folks went to the white church; they had a place for you to sit. After Freedom, there wasn't but one colored church, and that was at Bluff Springs.

I live right in the house now that I lived in when I was a slave. I was born in Murfreesboro, but we was moved down here when I was about six or eight weeks old. Mother took the pneumonia and died. I been right here ever since.

The white folks sold one colored woman, to send their boy to school to be a doctor. I remember it as well as if it was yesterday. They sold her away from her husband. They carried her on down in Mississippi. My marster owned seventeen or twenty heads of slaves. He wasn't cruel to his nigger hands.

I had a brother who would always slip off, and the patterollers would run him many a night. Right up under the house he would go, and they couldn't get to him. They come there some five or six times trying to catch him, and then they went to the house and called Marster and told him to call his nigger out so they could give him a genteel whipping and make him stay at home. But Marster told them he would whip him in the morning. Brother was laying right there listening, and he knowed right then he wasn't gonna get a whipping. The next morning when Marster got done eating his breakfast, he called Brother and said, "Well, I reckon I better see after you this morning. Haven't I told you to stop running around at night? I hope they catch you some night. Then you will stay in."

His mammy and him, neither one wasn't cruel to his

colored people. They got a new overseer once, and he overheard Mistress say to one of the slaves, "I'm gonna have you whipped if you ever do anything again." He got the slave and whipped her 'til he cut the blood out of her shoulder. He made her undo her clothes and whipped her. Mistress saw the blood on her and asked her what was the matter, and she told her that the overseer had whipped her. She called him and told him to never whip another one of her slaves again that way, and that she didn't believe in whipping them like that. That made him mad, and he said he wasn't gonna fool with any of them again.

Marster died three years after Freedom. After so many years, I married, and me and my wife bought the place from Mistress where I live now. Money was hard to get then, too, but Mistress 'lowed me a chance to pay for it.

All of my folks dead now—white and black. That tells me that my time ain't long off.

My father was a shoemaker. That was his trade. He hardly ever done any work in the fall of the year but made shoes. People would bring him leather, and he would keep busy plumb up to Christmas. Everybody around brought him leather. He made fine ones and coarse ones, and he made then all by hand. Now it is done by machines. He charged them so much for making them. The white folks didn't have nothing to do with what he charged. I can't say much about my father. They told me his father was a white man. He proved that he was right smart kin to the other race, by his hair and build and everything.

I knew I was a slave after I got big enough to know that I couldn't do the things that I wanted to do. Mrs. James had a sister from the North to come visit her, and she would talk to my father, and she told him once that in a short time he would be free as she was, and told him not to tell what she had told him, but that Lincoln was going to free all the slaves. I have heard a heap of colored people say that all white folks was just alike. That ain't so, 'cause there is some white folks will treat you right, and some will take everything away from you. They ain't all just alike.

I used to be a great fiddler. I first learned how to play on a long gourd with horsehair strings on it. Course, I couldn't go very high on it, but it done pretty well. That was the first of my learning to play. After a while, I bought me a fiddle for $1.80, and after so long a time I bought me a fiddle sure enough.

It wasn't but one family of free niggers up here. White people didn't recognize them, and they didn't 'low niggers to go around them. If they knowed they went around them, they would cut they backs off nearly. The men woulda noticed the slave girls if the white folks woulda let them. But they wouldn't let the girls go with a free Negro.

They had a riot here in '74. The white folks was treating the colored folks so bad that they said they was gonna put a stop to it. Four or five of them was killed, and it made the white folks so mad that they wanted to kill up all the niggers in the county, and seemed like they almost done it, from the amount that was killed in that riot.

When Freedom come along, Master come out one Monday morning and said, "Well, boys, you-all is just as free as I am this morning." Nigger was wondering what he was going to do, for he still had to look to the white man, for he didn't know what to do with hisself.

They had a debate here some time ago—some said colored folks was better off in slavery, and some said they wasn't. They have more privileges now, in some things anyhow. I'd rather be out of slavery than in, all the time.

# I Lived on Gallatin Pike

*I* was born in Nashville. I's up in ninety years, but I tell them I's still young. I lived on Gallatin Pike long 'fore the war and used to see the soldiers ride by.

My marster's name was William Penn Harding. My daddy was sold at Sparta, Tennessee, 'fore I was born, and Marster Harding bought him. My mammy already belonged to the Hardings.

When the fighting got so heavy, my white people got some Irish people to live on the plantation, and they went south, leaving us with the Irish people.

I was little, and I guess I didn't think much 'bout Freedom. I'd always had plenty to eat and wear. Our white folks didn't whip my people, but the overseers whipped the slaves on other plantations.

The Yankees had camps on the Capitol Hill [in Nashville]. And there was soldier camps in East Nashville, and you had to have a pass to get through.

I went to school at Fisk a short time, when it was near Twelfth and Cedar, and awhile down on Church Street. My teacher always bragged on me for being clean and neat. I didn't get much schooling. My daddy was like most folks. He thought if'n you knowed your ABC's and could read a line, that was enough. And he hired me out. Don't know what they paid me, for it was paid to my daddy.

I was hired to a Mrs. Ryan for years, where the Loveman store is now. There was a theater where Montgomery Ward store is. A lot of the theater people roomed and boarded with Mrs. Ryan, and they would give me passes to the show, and I'd slip in the gallery and watch the show. I couldn't read a word, but I enjoyed going. My daddy was a driver for Mr. Ryan.

I nursed for a Mrs. Mitchell, and she had a boy in school. One summer day, she went away. A Mrs. Smith with ten boys wanted me to stay with her 'til Mrs. Mitchell got back, and I stayed and liked them so well that I wouldn't go back to Mrs. Mitchell.

I went to Memphis and married George Grisham in 1870. He joined the army as bandleader, went to San Antonio, Texas, and I come back to Mrs. Smith's and stayed 'til her mammy lost her mind. My husband died in Texas, from heart trouble. All his things was sent back to me, and every month I got a thirty-dollar pension for me and my daughter. When she was sixteen, they cut it down, and I only get twelve dollars now.

I educated my daughter at Fisk, and she's been teaching school since 1893. She buy this place, and we live together. We have food, health, and both is happy. I have a woman come every Monday and wash for us.

# White Folks Raised Me

Yes, I was here in slavery then. It is pretty nearly left me now, but I know a whole lot. I was sold when I was nine years old. I never had no mother or father; white folks raised me. I was sold. Wilson County on the Woods Ferry Road. Yes, I have been through a heap. The Lawd has sho' spared me.

They sold a heap of colored people. They passed right by here, taking them to Nashville sale house. A whole lot of them was sent to Mississippi. I didn't have to go to Mississippi. So many people what I knowed went to Mississippi. I had a daddy, and he had to go. My daddy was sold and sent to Mississippi when I was a little bitty girl. I never did get to see him again. A old man took me up to the graveyard on

Gallatin Road, and we stayed all day, but we never did find my father's grave. I never did find it, but Uncle Charlie told me he was killed over on Rangers Hill. I don't know where that was, but they buried the soldiers what was killed that day out on Gallatin Road, white and black together. I don't know what his name was when he went to Mississippi, but I looked for him. I knew his name before he left, but I don't know who he belonged to in Mississippi.

I have been in the white folks' hands ever since I was so high. They took me in the white folks' house and kept me there 'til after the war, and if I went to any colored folks' house I had to come back 'fore night. I cleaned up and toted water and scrubbed and washed dishes—I have washed dishes a long time—and done anything they asked me to. But when my mother died, I was just throwed away, 'cause she took care of me. I had a half-sister and a half-brother, but they is dead.

I used to have a tin pan and a tin cup. Down on the floor, that's where I ate.

After the war, I begun to get out amongst people, but before the war I better not go out the house. No'm, go to nothing, corn shuckings or nothing. They'd have corn shuckings all around in the neighborhood, but I better not say nothing. Yes'm, I was the only one stayed in the house, and I don't reckon I would've stayed in there, but my mother died, and after she died I was a little baby, and they took me right in the house. The day of the sale, the young mist'ess bought me.

No'm, my master was his own overseer. He wouldn't have an overseer. They beat the darkies too much, and he wanted to beat his own. He used to beat them right smart. I used to remember about him whipping them. I don't know much about colored folks before the war. I wasn't 'lowed to go to see them. I better not be seen talking to colored people; they would whip me. I couldn't talk to the Negroes in the kitchen.

I slept with ole Mist'ess 'til I was too big and used to kick her, and then they made me a pallet on the floor, and I never stayed in her bed anymore. She told Mary, her daughter, to make me a tick and let me sleep on the floor. The girl said, "Why?" and she said, "She kicked me. I didn't sleep a bit last night." And she got some straw, and I slept right by her bed. When she died, they wrote me a letter, and I didn't go. That was after the war. They had treated me so bad I wouldn't go back. We lived right on the Stuart Ferry Road. I don't remember but one sister, and she died right after the war.

When the war came, all of them ran away and came to Nashville. Nobody stayed but Uncle Charlie. I had to stay. I stayed in the white folks' house, and they wouldn't let me out of the house without some of the white children with me. Oh, yes, I could just see the cannons when they were shooting. And my mist'ess, she wouldn't 'low me to stay in the yard, and one day I was on the fence, and some Yankee soldier came and said something to me, and she didn't 'low me out on the fence anymore. She said, "They will kill us."

The war ceasted two years after I stayed there, and they put me out and told me to go on, they was tired of giving me anything, and to go on and work for myself. And I started working for some white people, for John Paul and

Anne Ridley. And she had a baby and died before she got up, and he took the baby to his mother, and that broke them up.

When Dr. Bradden came here after the war, my brother and Uncle Charlie begged me to go to school and learn, but the white folks had beat all the learning out of me. And Uncle Charlie said that if I got old I certainly would hate it, and I sho' do.

All my white folks dead now. Ain't none of them living. The old man what brought me butter and milk told me all of them is gone and none of them is living. I never have been up there since I lived up there. He said the boy had built a nice house, and he said he was dead, too. They wouldn't have no houses built like those that was log. They had wide planks on it, and cement put in there. He said I wouldn't know the place if I was to see it, 'cause it is so much different from what it was.

# I Would Die Fighting Rather Than Be a Slave Again

Robert Falls

If I had my life to live over, I would die fighting rather than be a slave again. I want no man's yoke on my shoulders no more. But in them days, us niggers didn't know no better. All we knowed was work, and hard work. We was learned to say, "Yes, sir!" and scrape down and bow and to do just exactly what we was told to do. Make no difference if we wanted it or not. Old Marster and old Mistress would say, "Do this!" and we done it. And they say, "Come here!" and if we didn't come to them they come to us, and they brought the bunch of switches with them.

They didn't half feed us either. They fed the animals better. They gives the mules roughage and such to chaw on all night, but they didn't give us nothing to chaw on. Learned us to steal, that's what they done. Then we would take anything we could lay our hands on, when we was hungry. Then they'd whip us for lying when we say we don't know nothing about it. But it was easier to stand when the stomach was full.

Now my father, he was a fighter. He was mean as a bear. He was so bad to fight and so troublesome [that] he was sold four times to my knowing, and maybe a heap more times. That's how come my name is Falls, even if some does call me Robert Goforth. Niggers would change to the name of their new marster every time they was sold. And my father had a lot of names but kept the one of his marster when he got a good home. That man was Barry Falls. He said he'd been trying to buy Father for a long time, because he was the best wagoner in all that country abouts.

My mother was sold three times before I was born. The last time, when old Goforth sold her to the slave speculators—you know, every time they needed money, they would sell a slave—and they was taking them, driving them just like a pack of mules, to the market from North Carolina into South Carolina, she began to have fits. You see, they had sold her away from her baby. They got to the jailhouse where they was to stay that night, and she took on so that the slave speculators couldn't do nothing with her. Next morning, one of them took her back to Marster Goforth and told him, "Look here, we can't do nothing with this woman. You got to take her and give us back our money. And do it now." And they mean it, too. So old Marster Goforth took my mother and give them back their money. After that, none of us was ever separated. We all lived, a brother and two sisters and my mother, with the Goforths 'til Freedom.

Marster Goforth counted himself a good old Baptist Christian. The one good deed he did, I never will forget—he made us all go to church every Sunday. That was the only place off the farm we ever went. Every time a slave went off the place, he had to have a pass, except we didn't for church. Everybody in that country knowed that the Goforth niggers didn't have to have a pass to go to church. But that didn't make no difference to the patterollers. They'd hide in the bushes or wait along the side of the road, and when the niggers come from meeting, the patterollers say, "Where's your pass?" Us Goforth niggers used to start running soon as we get out of church. We never got caught.

Old Marster was too old to go to the war. He had one son was a soldier, but he never come home again. I never seen a soldier 'til the war was over and they begin to come back to the farms. We half-grown niggers had to work the farm, because all the farmers had to give I believe it was a tenth of their crops to help feed the soldiers.

It was a long time before we knowed we was free. Then one night, old Marster come to our house, and he say he wants to see us all before breakfast tomorrow morning, and to come over to his house. He got something to tell us. Next morning, we went over there. I was the monkey, always acting smart. I just spoke sassy like and say, "Old Marster, what you got to tell us?"

My mother said, "Shut your mouth, fool. He'll whip you!"

And old Marster say, "No, I won't whip you. Never no more. Sit down there, all of you, and listen to what I got to tell you. I hates to do it, but I must. You ain't all my niggers no more. You is free. Just as free as I am. I have raised you-all to work for me, and now you are going to leave me. I am an old man, and I can't get along without you. I don't know what I am going to do."

Well, sir, it killed him. He was dead in less than ten months.

Everybody left right now but me and my brother and another fellow. Old Marster fooled us to believe we was duty-bound to stay with him 'til we was all twenty-one. But my brother, that boy was stubborn. Soon he say he ain't going to stay there. And he left. In about a year, maybe less, he come back, and he told me I didn't have to work for old Goforth. I was free, sure enough free. And I went with him, and he got me a job railroading. But the work was too hard for me. I couldn't stand it. So I left there and went to my mother. I had to walk. It was forty-five miles. I made it in a day. She got me work there where she worked.

I remember so well how the roads was full of folks walking and walking along when the niggers was freed. Didn't know where they was going, just going to see about something else somewhere else. Meet a body in the road. "Where you going?"

"Don't know."

"What you going to do?"

"Don't know."

And then sometimes we would meet a white man, and he would say, "How would you like to come work on my farm?"

And we say, "I don't know."

And then maybe he say, "If you come work for me on my farm, when the crops is in, I give you five bushels of corn, five gallons of molasses, some ham meat, and all your clothes and vittles while you works for me."

All right! That's what I could do. And then something begins to work up here [points to his head]. I begins to think then I could make a living for my own self, and I never had to be a slave no more.

# I Remember the Yankee Soldiers Well

Frances Batson

*I* don't know just how old I is. I was born here in Nashville during slavery. I must be way past ninety, for I remember the Yankee soldiers well. The chillun called them the "Blue Mans."

My white folks was named Crockett. Dr. Crockett was our marster, but I don't remember him myself. He died when I was small. My marster was mean to my mammy when her older chillun would run away. My older brother went to war with my marster. My younger brother run away. They caught him, took him home, and whipped him. He run away and was never found.

We wasn't sold, but my mammy went away and left me. When I got up one mornin' and went to Mammy's room, she was gone. I cried and cried for her. My missus wouldn't let me outside the house for fear I'd try to find her.

After Freedom, my brother and a Yankee soldier come in a wagon to get us. My white folks said, "I don't see why you is takin' those chillun."

My brother said, "We is free now."

I remember one whipping my missus give me. Me and her daughter slipped away to the river to fish. We caught a fish, and my missus had it cooked for us but whipped us for going to the river.

Where the Buena Vista School is used to be a Yankee soldiers' barrack. Every morning, they had music. We chillun would go on the hill where the big mill is now and listen to them. I remember a black horse the soldiers had, that if you called him Jeff Davis he would run you.

I remember the old well on Cedar Street near the capitol, and six mules fell in it. That was back when blackberries was growing on the Capitol Hill. In Morgan Park was called the "Pleasure Garden." And it was full of Yankee soldiers. After the war, was so many German people over here that from Jefferson Street to Clay Street was called "Dutch Town."

Since Freedom, I've hired out, washed and cooked for different people. My mammy used to tell me how the white folks would hire the slaves out to make money for the marster, and she told me some of the marsters would hide their slaves to keep the Yankees from getting them.

I don't believe in white-and-black marriages. My sister married a light man. I wouldn't marry one if it would turn me to gold.

Don't know nothing 'bout voting. That was for the men.

These young peoples is tough. I think half of them'll be hung. The way they throw rocks at ole people—that's why I'm crippled now. A white boy hit me with a rock.

# I Could Hear the Bullets Flying All Around

Name unknown

*I* was a slave until I was twelve years old. I married two years after I come here. I married when I was fourteen years old. I had six children and raised them without a husband. I been a widow forty years. All my children died, but they got grown and married before they died. I ain't got no people at all. Nobody but me here. Three of my daughters died inside of three years. My last son owned this home. I had one granddaughter. She died with consumption. She was the only grandchild I had. Nobody in the world but me.

Well, my old marster was named Billy Shaw. He was a Methodist preacher. He didn't do us like he was a preacher, though. I was born in Robertson County. They moved us here in covered wagons. My mother was sold from me, and they kept me. They sold her to some people here in town. My old marster was right good to us—that is, he wasn't as mean as some of them was. He would knock and beat us. Lord, I said if I ever got away from that place I would never go back again.

Yes, ma'am, he was mean to them slave women, even if he was going with them. If his wife find it out, he would have to sell her. He would sell his own children by slave women just like he would any others, just since he was making money. In slavery, niggers and mules was white folks' living. They would sell for five hundred dollars and a thousand dollars. My mother sold for a thousand dollars.

I belonged to my marster's daughter. I just had to knock around the best way I could until my mother sent for me. They hired me out when I was only six years old. They said they hired me out to pick up things after the child and see after her. But they carried me to the cornfield and put a bucket on my arm, and I dropped corn all day in the hot sun. If I missed any rows, he would take the hoe and beat me. I had to go just as fast as he could. If he got to the end before I could get there, well, I would get a beating. They made me tote fodder after night. They made me go out there after night with them men. Sometimes we would tote it all night. I used to hear runaway niggers running in the field at night.

My old marster used to have a lot of slaves before his son broke him. But after he got broke, he didn't have many. I don't know whether his son broke him while he was running on the river, or some other way. They sold my mother but not me. They would let me come to see my mother sometimes and stay three or four days. The white folks I stayed with treated me so mean that my mother got a man to slip me away from them. He brought me on here to her. He come and got me about twelve or one o'clock in the night. He told me he was coming to get me. They brought me here to the Picketts', here in town. They was talking about sending me south, but if they had done that I would never have got to see my mother.

I never heard my mother say she went to camp meeting but once in my life. They wouldn't let them have church. My mother was married in Robertson County. Her marster married her. He was a squire. Her father come from Clarksville. He was a carpenter. His name was Jack Hale. He belonged to a man named Hale down in Clarksville.

When a slave got ready to marry, he would just come to the marster and tell him that he wanted one of his women, and he could just take her. They didn't have no ceremony. They wouldn't let a scrubby man come in among them, but if he was healthy he could just take her and start living with her. They jump over the broomstick in them days. I never seed nobody marry until I was free. If a neighbor's man got a child by your woman, that was your child. He couldn't take it away. When your marster had a baby born in his family, they would call all the niggers and tell them to come in and "see your new marster." We had to call them babies "Mister" and "Miss," too.

They would hire the nigger children out to work, then they could sell them. I used to hoe cotton just like a man.

If anybody had corn they wanted to get shucked, well, they would give corn shuckings. They said they had a good time. Anyhow, that was the only good time they had. They would pass around cider to them. The women would have quiltings.

They would have little suppers sometimes at the quiltings. They would have dances sometimes and turn a pot upside down right in front of the door. They said that would keep the sound from going outside. Look like people had better times in some things than they do now. But their good times was so long between times. At Christmas, they would let them have a little fun. But that was just on Christmas Day.

Yes, I can remember the war. When I was out in Flat Rock, I could hear the bullets flying all around, just whizzing by. The Yankees would come and take everything they wanted—corn, horses, and anything they wanted. They would have brought me to town, but I was afraid to come. I just stayed out there until my mother sent for me. I lived down in a little house all by myself. Nobody never bothered me. My uncle fought in the war. There was a lot of colored men fought in the war. There was a lot of fighting all up and down the Franklin Pike. The Maxwell House was the barracks. They would bring the wounded soldiers there. I was living right on Cherry Street Pike. If the Rebel soldiers would come, well, I would have to go and cook them something good to eat.

After the war, niggers would run away, two and three every night. That's the way they got away after they was free. After you run away and they would catch you, they would put you in the calaboose until your marster would come and get you out.

Lord, yes, I was here when they lynched Eph Grizzard. Some of them say he got away, that when he was throwed over the bridge they didn't look to see his body, but that some doctor helped him get away to Kansas.

# My Daddy Was Part Indian

*I* was born in Murfreesboro on Stones River. I don't know how old I is, and it would make me 'shamed to tell people that, but my mammy would hit me in the mouth when I'd ask how old I was. She say I was just trying to be grown.

My mammy's name was Frankie, and my daddy was Henry Ken Kannon. Don't remember much about Mammy 'cept she was a short, fat Indian woman with a terrible temper. She died during the war, with black measles. My daddy was part Indian and couldn't talk plain. When he go to the store, he'd have to put his hand on what he wanted to buy. He died eight months 'fore the centennial. Our marster and missus was Landon and Sweenie Ken Kannon. They was good to us, and we had good things to eat.

I remember the Yankee and Southern soldiers. One day,

me and my young missus and some chillun went up the road, and we seed some Yankee soldiers coming. I climbed on the fence. The others ran away and hid. One of the soldiers says to me, "Little girl, who was that with you?"

And I says, "It was Miss Puss and some chillun."

He laughed and says, "You is brave, ain't you?"

Our missus let us go to church. I belong to the Church of Christ.

I don't know but one slave that got land or nothing when Freedom was declared. We didn't get nothing at Freedom. My daddy went back in the woods and built us a sapling house and daubed it with mud. After Freedom, my daddy went away, and we chillun stayed in that house in the woods by ourselves. There was two weeks we didn't see a bit of bread. I went up what is called the Nine-Mile Cut near Tullahoma and asked a woman if she would let us have some bread. She give me some meat and bread and told me to come back. I went back home, and we ate something, and I went back to the woman's house. She give me a sack of flour and a big piece of middlin' meat. We was scared being there alone, so I would set up while my brothers slept, then I'd sleep in the daytime. One night, somebody knocked at the door, and it was my daddy, and he had two sacks of food, and the other chillun got up, and we ate a big meal.

I didn't go to school. My daddy wouldn't let me. Said he needed me in the field more than I needed school. I was always sassy and stubborn. I run away from my daddy and come to Nashville. I stayed at a school on Franklin Pike run by Mrs. McGathey. I was the only colored person there. They was good to me, and every Christmas I would get a big box of clothes and things.

In Manchester, the Ku Klux Klan wore big, high hats, red handkerchiefs on their faces, and red covers on their horses. They took two niggers out of jail and hung them from a chestnut tree.

One night when I was going with my daddy from the field house, we met some of the KKK, and they said, "Ain't you out late, Henry? And who is that gal with you?"

My daddy said, "We is going home from work, and this is my daughter."

They said, "Where has she been? We ain't never seed her."

He told them I'd been in Nashville. They said they'd be back that night, but we didn't see them.

When I was in Manchester, I prómised the Lawd I wouldn't dance. But one night, I was on the ball floor dancing from one end of the room to the other, and something says to go to the door. I didn't go right then, and again it says, "You is not keeping your promise." I went to the door, and you could pick a pin off the ground, it was so light. In the sky was the prettiest thing you ever seed, so many colors—blue, white, green, red, and yellow.

Since Freedom, I's worked with different people, cooking and keeping house. I's the mammy of three chillun. Two of them is away from here, and I live with my daughter.

When I used to go to camp meetings, they had big dinners and spread it on the ground. They preached, sung, shouted, and everybody had a good time. From the camp meetings, they would go to the wharf and baptize. They would tie handkerchiefs round their heads. When they was dipped under the water, some of them would come up shouting.

One time, the preacher was in the river fixing to baptize a man. Everybody was singing "Ole-Time Religion." A woman sang, "I don't like that thing behind you."

'Bout that time, the parson and the other man seed an alligator. The parson says, "No, by God, I don't either." He turned the man loose, and they both ran away.

# All My Bosses Were Nigger Traders

Name unknown

*I* wasn't very old when the Civil War began. I had just turned into my sixteenth year. I remember when the Yankees come to this town. My old boss hit me that mornin', and he didn't know the Yankees were in town, and when he found it out he come back beggin' me to stay with him, and said he was sorry.

We were living one and a half miles from the depot. All my bosses were nigger traders 'til they married, and then they settled down. I've seen them sell women away from little children, and women would be crying, and they'd slap 'em about crying. I've seen droves of slaves come through, all chained together. And I laughed; I didn't known no better.

I belonged to Jim Caruthers. He was a good man, and he had about one hundred darkies. I was just a little motherless child, kicked and knocked about.

When I was on the farm, I was not big enough to do much. I could chop cotton, but I was quite young. I was sick once, and Dr. Clifford said, "Let him eat anything he wants, 'cause he can't be raised." Marster told old Missus if she could raise me she could have me, and she took me in the house with her and nursed me 'til I got well.

There wasn't but one family of half-white chillun on our place. The old lady would be meaner to them than she was to the black ones. Some of them was Marster's chillun, and old Mistress would not have one of them for a house servant. She would get one right black and wouldn't have none of them in there looking as white as her.

We had beef soup, cabbage, beans, and things like that for dinner. Of course, we had meat and bread for breakfast. But you could go in the cellar and get all the meal you wanted. We stole so many chickens that if a chicken would see a darky he'd run right straight to the house.

I always wanted some boots, and one old lady said, "If you'll kill me a pig, I'll get you a boot." I give her three or four pigs, but I never did get no boots. Oh, yes, 'long in the fall, he'd give his darkies shoes, and he'd have 'em half-soled once a year. We'd get a coat every other year, and he'd give you a full suit and two pair of pants that winter. And he'd give you two coarse cotton shirts to carry you through the winter. Little children wore what their parents put on 'em.

They'd have to shuck corn at night when they'd come from the field. There was so many of them on our place it wouldn't take 'em no later than ten o'clock to get through. I've been to many a corn shucking at night, five miles from here. There was a crowd from Big Harper and a crowd from Little Harper, and after we got through the shucking they'd give us whiskey, and there'd be plenty of fighting, and the Little Harper white folks would take up for their darkies, and the Big Harper white folks would do the same. I used to think them was the best times. They had some kind of biscuit mixed with sweet potatoes, and I thought it was the best eating. They would have a big dance, too, and often after the dance they would go to fighting.

Slavery was not such a bad time for me. I was young, and my mother and father died when I was real young. We'd play marbles and run rabbits, and there was always eighty or ninety little chillun on our place. They had an old woman there to look after them—one that had broke down. When company would come, they would put clothes on them and march them up to the house so they could see his little niggers. We was afeared to go up to the house.

I remember once he built a house for young Marster, and he said he was gonna let the darkies have a dance there, and they thought he was, sure 'nough. But he didn't, so they decided to have a dance anyhow. It was a moonlight night, and they had this big dance in the field, and the patterollers come and caught one man and throw him right on me, and he come and got me and said, "Goddamn you," and kept his hand right in my collar and held me home to Marster. He told Marster that he had told me that if I would tell who-all was there he wouldn't whip me, but if I didn't he would whip me all daylight. And you ought to heard me telling! It was around the time when the niggers was rising, and they asked me did I hear them shooting: "Did you see any guns?"

And I said, "No, I didn't see no guns, but I heard them shooting." I hadn't heard a thing, but I knowed what they wanted to hear, so I said I did.

They caught Tom Hodge, too, and he had to tell. I couldn't go to none of the parties after that. The niggers would kick me out if they saw me; they wouldn't have me there.

I've seen 'em handcuffed long as from here to the fence out there, women screaming and hollering about leaving their chillun. Yes, I've seen many a [runaway slave], and darkies would help 'em round. The Mississippi niggers in our camp used to get to talking, and they told once about a man named Bullens who had hounds trained to catch the niggers, and they would tree you and carry you back. They say that when anybody would come for the hounds to run a nigger, the hounds would say, "Our Father, I've got a heavenly home up yonder, hallelujah, hallelujah."

When I went to the war, I was turning seventeen. I was in the Battle of Nashville, when we whipped old Hood. I went to see my mistress on my furlough, and she was glad to see me. She said, "You remember when you were sick and I had to bring you to the house and nurse you?"

And I told her, "Yes'm, I remember."

And she said, "And now you are fighting me!"

I said, "No'm, I ain't fighting you. I'm fighting to get free."

I have buried many a man out in that cemetery on the Murfreesboro Pike. We had so many to bury a day, and we had to wait 'til the wagon would bring 'em in, and then we would put 'em on our shoulders and take him and bury him. You could hear men cussing and saying, "Somebody's got my man." They would hide him and go off to see the girls and then come back, going to bury him late that night, and somebody would steal him and bury him. I couldn't do that now.

I never got 'rested but once, and that was in the war.

The first battle the colored ever got into was Fort Pillow [in Tennessee]; they buried some of them colored soldiers alive. Then when they went to Mobile, Alabama, they would just shoot 'em down, and they would just say that he broke to run, and they had to shoot him to keep him from getting away. They'd do that anytime they got afraid that they would run into the Yankees and they would take the nigger prisoners from them. I saw 'em hanging the Rebels right there in the penitentiary during the war. They tried to hang everyone that was in that battle [Fort Pillow], for the way they done the colored soldiers. I saw 'em captured just as barefooted, and it was snow on the ground. I've been right to the bridge, where I was a guard. When the Yankees got near Nashville, the niggers started running to 'em.

I'd been better off if I'd bought in the country. I married when I was twenty-one years old, and I didn't owe but seven dollars on my place. I always wanted a home and a gun, and I got both of them, but my boy took my gun when they had the riot in St. Louis, and I never did buy another one.

Some of them say they don't see why I vote for the Yankees; they say they didn't do nothing for me. But I tell 'em the Yankees done 'nough when they set me free.

I had two sisters, and they were sent off, and there was

three brothers. My sisters were given to my young mistress when she married. My sister was carried away from me, and I went to see her 'rectly after the war. I thought she was dead after that visit, but I met a tramp one day, and he said he was from Sheffield, Alabama. I told him I used to have a sister there, and he asked me what was her name, and I told him, and he said, "I saw her yesterday."

I said, "You're lying. She's been dead for years."

But he told me all about them and told it so straight—and how many chillun she had and everything—that I went to see her. And she was ninety-eight years old, and we had a sure-'nough meeting. She was so glad to see me, and she told everybody, "That's my youngest brother."

My sister that's living now stays up on Locklayer in Nashville. She's eighty-four. Clay Farmer lives in that same neighborhood, too. We was boys together. Yes, his marster was a very nice old man. One of his men married a sister of mine, but he was unruly, and they had to sell him to Mississippi. Yes, he would fight—fight white and colored, too.

I got two sons, and they never give me any trouble. One is in St. Louis, working in the post office, and the other is at the Andrew Jackson Building in Nashville. My daughter lives in my other house out on the highway.

# Sometime She Would Lock Us Up in a Dark Closet

Cecilia Chappel

*I* was born in Marshall County, Tennessee. I'm the oldest of two chillun, and I'm 102 years old. I feels like I've been here longer than that. My mammy was brought to Nashville and sold to some people that took her to Mississippi to live.

My marster and missus was named Bob and Nancy Lord. Every slave had to say "Missus" and "Marster," and also to the white babies. I still says it. And if I come to your door, I never comes in 'til you ask me. Lots of my folks says to me that I is too ole-fashion, and I says I don't care. I was raised with manners and too ole to change.

Our marster give us good food and clothes. I was learnt how to knit, weave, sew, and spin. On rainy days, we was given a certain ’mount of weavin’ to do and had to get it done.

I don’t know how to read or write. The white folks didn’t ’low us to learn nothing. I declare, you better not get caught with a paper in your hand. If I had half a chance like you chillun have, I’d go to bed with my books.

Our marster ’lowed us to go to church. I went barefoot and had a rag tied round my head, and my dress come up to my knees. That preacher man would get up there and tell us, “Now, you mind your marster and missus and don’t steal from them.”

I stayed with Missus for a long time after I got Freedom, and I cried like a fool when I had to leave them. My missus says, “You is just as free as I is,” but I always had good clothes and good food, and I didn’t know how I’d get them after I left her.

My white folks was tight on us, but ole as I is, I often think that they never hit a lick that I didn’t need. If’n they hadn’t raised me right, I might have go in meanness [turned mean] and been locked up half the time. But I ain’t never been ’rested, and I’s ’fraid of the policemen.

The field slaves was whipped in the fields by the overseer, and the marster and missus did it at the house. I tell you, we had a hard time. My missus wouldn’t let them sell me. I was a nurse and house girl. I was whipped with a bullwhip and got cuts on my back many a time. I’s not ashamed to say I got scars on my back now from Marster cutting it with that bullwhip. My missus also whipped me. When the missus got ready to whip me, she would give us some work to do, so she would kind of get over her spell

’fore she whipped us. Sometimes she would lock us up in a dark closet and bring our food to us. I hated being locked up.

After they took me out of the house, I worked in the field like the others. Long ’fore daybreak, we was standing in the fields leaning on our hoes, waiting for daylight and waiting for the horn to blow so we could start work.

If’n we wanted to go to anyplace, we had to have a pass with our marster’s name on it, and if you didn’t have it you got tore to pieces, and then your marster tore you up when you got home.

One story my daddy used to tell us was ’bout a slave named Pommpy. He was always praying for the good Lord to take him away. One night, he was down on his knees praying, “Good Lord, come and take po’ Pommpy out of his misery.” The marster of Pommpy heared him and made a little noise, and Pommpy says, “Who is that?”

And his marster says, “It’s the Lord come to take po’ Pommpy out of his misery.”

Pommpy crawl under the bed and says, “Pommpy has been gone two or three days.”

Since Freedom, I have nursed, cooked, and done different things. I worked for one family fifteen years and didn’t miss a day. I has stayed at this place for the last five years. I had a stroke and was in the hospital a long time. I can’t get out. And round here in the house, I has to walk with a stick.

I ain’t never voted. One day, some men come here to take me to vote. I told them when I got ready to be a man I would put on overalls.

I’s a member of the Missionary Baptist Church. I ain’t

been for a long time 'cause I ain't able to go.

Oh Lawdy! I think some of these young people ain't no-'count, while some of them is all right.

I think each color should marry his own color. It makes me mad to think about it. If the good Lawd had wanted that, he would have had us all one color.

For a long time, the Relief [Office] give me a quart of milk a day, but now all I has is what my sister Harriett give me. She ain't got much work, and some days we don't have much to eat. If my missus was living, I wouldn't go hungry.

# You Couldn't Go Nowhere without a Pass

*Sister:* I was born right here in this county. There wasn't none of those houses here then, neither the jailhouse or the courthouse. Just had horses and wagons and plenty of dust.

You couldn't go nowhere without a pass. Did, you would got your shirt took off and got a whipping.

Darkies would go to church after the white folks got through. You had to stay at home and cook dinner for them, and after everything was over you could go to the white folks' church.

My mother was a mother of ten children. My father was born free. They said his mother was a white woman. He didn't remember his father. He was free but lived right on the place with my mother, and she was a slave. He hired hisself out and had a little garden and a watermelon patch. On big days in town, my mother would always make some ginger cakes, and he would carry them on the square and sell them. Old Virginia was his home. He never did see his father.

The last count I had of my age, I reckon I am between 96 and 97 years old. My father lived to be 110 years old. I got 10 great-grandchildren.

❋

*Younger brother:* I will be seventy-three years old my next birthday. I remember when the Yankees come through stealing everything in sight. Young Master was in the war, and he used to slip back to see his people in the night to keep the Yankees from catching him. Many a night, you could hear them protectors [probably Union patrols] running around all night, looking for men who would slip off, and they would be right up there in bed 'sleep. I could hear them cannons way 'cross at Fort Pillow bellowing out. They would be so big that it would take twenty-five or thirty horses to pull them.

White folks used to have overseers riding up and down the field to see that you would keep working. If they caught you loafing, they would tie your hands with a chain or anything like that and whip you. Master sent our older sister off down to Mississippi. He slipped her off at night, but Mother couldn't do nothing 'bout it but set down and cry. They would drive slaves off just like they do hogs now. A great big nigger like me would bring four or five thousand dollars, but a little nigger wouldn't bring nothing hardly. Nobody didn't want a little puny nigger. Our white folks wasn't so good and wasn't so mean.

There was one or two families of free niggers around. Sarah Powell was free all her days. We used to call her "Free Sarah." She hired herself out to the white folks.

We wore good clothes 'cause Mammy spun and wove them. We wore brogan shoes with brass tips on them. Mammy would knit our socks; she would have one strand of wool and one strand of cotton. Mammy was the cook, and she would do all the weaving.

❋

*Older brother:* I was born in 1854. I toted water during the war. Me and old Master's daughter used to play together all the time, and one day we was out in the field playing together and old boss come out and slapped her jaws and give me a hoe, and from that time on I was in the field. Guess he thought I had got big enough to work then. Master just had one man outside of our family. It was thirteen of us. Every one of us lived together and got grown before any of the family died. Father was born before the Revolutionary War. He was 104 when he died.

Sometimes I think we was a little better off then than now. Then we didn't have to worry 'bout nothing to eat and wear, and now it is a little tough on you, and making no money either.

I remember just as well when Master come out one morning and said, "Well, you-all is just as free as I is this morning." He didn't tell us 'til a year after Freedom was declared, though.

I said, "We been knowing it all the time but just been waiting for you to tell us."

He said, "I want you-all to stay with me if you will."

When Christmas come, he made my oldest brother drunk and said he would give us seven hundred dollars if we would stay, and my brother made the deal. But we done well if we got seventy-five dollars out of it. He just made promises.

Master hired my mother out a whole year, and she didn't get a thing for it. Old Master borrowed from my father, and he owed me a thousand dollars. The Yankees camped near where we lived, and I found a roll of money that they had dropped as big as my arm. Master said he was going to send it back and get some good money for me, and I never got none of it at all.

If a boy went with a girl and spoke things that he shouldn't, he could get a whipping for that. If you fooled a girl up and got her with a armful, you had to take care of her. Now a boy can beat a girl up nearly to death and don't tell their mother nothing. I heard one slap a girl out here the other night, and her jaw was all swelled up the next morning like she had a egg in it. And she made out like she had the toothache.

I ain't no married man. I don't see nobody I want. I'm 'fraid to marry anybody, for I reckon all the good ones been taken. Guess I'll have to order one from Sears and Roebuck.

They have college preachers now. They don't have religion like they used to. I saw old man George Jones do a thing one day that I never seen before or since. Right down here in the Methodist church one Sunday, he got happy and actually flew around the altar. Not a foot nor a hand was touching the floor. I believe he was really a Christian.

# I Don't Never Want to See Another War

Liza Reynolds

*I* got three children dead, and I ain't got nobody now in the world living. I'm just by myself. My father got killed on the battlefield when I was three years old.

I got the little dress here now that I wore. I'll get it and show it to you. Here 'tis. Ain't it cute and little? My mother used to wash it every week, and I washed it after she died, 'til I got so I wasn't able to do it. My mother been dead forty-four years. It gives me a pleasure to look at this little dress. Look here at the lace where I tore it going to my mother asking her for tiddy. I never did sew it up 'cause she said I stepped in it going to her.

I have fed more white folks than anybody. They worked at Phillips and Buttorff's foundry, and my table was full all the time. I used to live right next door there and had a restaurant, but I got burnt out. I lost everything I had. Ain't even got clothes now. My legs got burnt, too. I used to feed from sixteen to eighteen white men for dinner. They come down here now to see me and say, "Aunt Liza, have you got anything to eat?"

I say, "No, I can't work now."

When I had a restaurant, I never turned a hobo down. If they would come in hungry, I would give them something to eat. I always had a big tableful. I had a big dish of hog head, a dish of fish, chitlins, and a big dish of chicken, and I always had plenty of cornbread and homemade light bread. I had just plenty of everything, and believe me I had the white people to eat with me. I remember one day a white man come up to me and shook me—I was sitting out in the yard, nodding—and said, "You don't know me, do you? Well, if you don't know me, you will know me. This is the old hobo." And he threw three silver dollars in my lap.

That woke me up good, and I said, "Name of God, who is this give me this money?"

Then he said, "Don't you remember the old hobo? This is him."

My young mistress is near about as old as me. She's got seven boys, and she lives at Morgantown, Tennessee.

Two men come here looking for me and wanted to know if my name was Liza Denton, and I told them that it used to be Denton, but I married a Reynolds. Me and my husband come to Murfreesboro and worked at the Jordan Hotel. I left there and brought my mother with me. She never seed a train 'til then. She never wore nothing but a sunbonnet, a gingham dress, and a white apron. I want to be like her. I want to go that way.

My mother had four children. That was all she ever had. I was the only girl. My mother had a good marster and mistress. I had my wrists burnt once when I was a child, and my mistress went to her grave with her hands so she couldn't shut them up, putting me out. Me and my brother was burning one another with broomsedge, and I caught fire and went running and hollering. My mistress caught me, and her arms stayed bent all the time. She used to say, "I wouldn't sell her for nothing. I wouldn't take less than a thousand dollars for him [Liza's brother], and I wouldn't take two thousand for her. That's my little breeder."

Mother said I cussed and said, "Damn you, I won't never be no breeder for you." I don't know how I learned to cuss.

They allowed us to have everything to eat they had. They had a big barrel of molasses propped up down in the cellar, and I tried to get some of it one day and pulled the barrel over on me and mashed my foot. Marster told Mistress, "Give them children enough molasses to eat. There's plenty of it here. They wouldn't have to steal it if you had give them enough." I oughta been whipped.

Ain't nobody seen the time I have seen. Old Mistress whipped the blood out of me just once. That was the only time she whipped me. Old Marster got a hickory stick and whipped her and said nobody ain't got no business with niggers if they don't know how to treat them. He told her if she whipped me again like that he would cut the blood out of her. He was so much better than she was.

Children then wasn't like they is now. Little girls know more now than I did after I got grown. I work all one day and a half in a hollow stump trying to find me a baby. When the doctor come around with the saddlebags, I told him to bring me a baby. I never knowed where they come from. They know now where they come from. I hear these little girls talking about their beaus now. They know more than I know.

They put my brother on the block and sold him off, and they carried him down south. I cried and cried 'til Marster's brother told me to hush crying, that he would go and get him tomorrow. I hushed for a while and break out crying again. But he went and got him and told his brother that he was going to pay for him hisself. He was a good man. He said he wasn't going to have that child crying for her brother.

I was baptized in Caney Fork River, with ice thick enough for wagons to roll over it. They broke the ice and throwed me under it. I have got that same old-time religion today. These children today ain't got the fire I got. None of them ain't raised. Go over there in that house. You can't see where it's never been swept in the world.

I don't never want to see another war. That one I saw was 'ragious. The Yankees would come in cussing and burn down fences and everything in sight as fast as they could. Yankees used to beat us, and we would dodge. Mother would take the baby and lay her in the cornfield to hide her and then lay down close by her. Mother would be listening. One of the soldiers said, "Don't hurt that little baby." The Yankees had my mother toting water half the night. They told her they wasn't going to hurt her little girl. They camped right there all night. My father belonged to Uncle Sam. He fought with the Yankees.

My husband been dead forty-five years. He died at Mount Pleasant. He was robbed and killed. Cut his throat.

When he sent word that he would be home one Saturday night, I had a big turkey. He was crazy about coons, and I had one, a big old-fashioned pound cake, and a white cake. And you could get a gallon of whiskey for a dollar then; I got that for him. I went down to the First Baptist Church and stayed 'til nearly twelve o'clock and said I must go on home, for if he was coming it was about time for him to be coming.

I hadn't been 'sleep long when Brother Huddleston, deacon of the church, come and knocked on the door. He talked so much like my husband I opened the door before I found out it wasn't him. He came in and said, "Uncle Hy can't come this Saturday 'cause he had so much work to do, but here is forty-nine dollars he sent you, and tell you enjoy yourself." But I was sorry he didn't come. I let the guests come on and let them eat the food anyway.

Just about daybreak, I heard somebody give one scream after another. Mrs. Solomon's husband got killed, and she wanted me to go to the depot with her. I didn't feel like going, for I felt bad all over. I looked up and saw the messenger boy coming, and fell over. The news come to me that my husband got killed.

Dr. Murphey worked with me three days, trying to get me to my senses.

I couldn't go where he was, 'cause smallpox was so bad

then they wouldn't let you out if you once got in there. He was a great big, fine, fat man. He was robbed of nineteen dollars.

My oldest brother died in Warren County. He had malaria fever. My other brother fell out of a tree and died. And my baby brother went away and come back and took pneumonia.

Young folks ain't got no manners now. One of the schoolboys up there pushed up against me and knocked me down, and he never did say nothing. I was feeling bad about it for three or four days. Brother Watson said he was going to see something about it. He was nice. He used to give me money often and come to see me.

# Folks These Days Don't Know What Trouble Looks Like

*O*ne thing that all wrong with this world today is that they ain't no prayer grounds. Down in Georgia where I was born—that was way back in 1852—us colored folks had prayer grounds. My mammy's was an old, twisted, thick-rooted muscadine bush. She'd go in there and pray for deliverance of the slaves. Some colored folks cleared out knee spots in the canebrakes. Cane, you know, grows high and thick, and colored folks could hide theirselves in there, and nobody could pester them.

You see, it was just like this. During the war, and before the war, too, white folks make a heap of fun of the colored folks for all the time praying. Sometimes, say you was a slave, and you get down to pray in the field or by the side of the road. White marster come along and see a slave on his knees. He say, "What you praying about?"

And you say, "Oh, Marster, I's just praying to Jesus 'cause I wants to go to Heaven when I dies."

And Marster says, "You is my Negro. I get you to Heaven. Get up off your knees."

The white folks what owned slaves thought that when they go to Heaven the colored folks would be there to wait on them.

And if a Yankee came along, he say, too, "What are you praying about?" You gives the same response. And he say, "We's going to save you. We going to set you free. You wants to be free, don't you?"

"Yes, sir, boss!"

"Well, then," Yank say, "come go along with me."

Ain't no use to keep saying, "Please, sir, boss, I'll have to ask my marster."

Yank say, "What you mean, 'marster'? You ain't got no marster. We's setting you free."

Sometimes they takes and ties a rope round you, and they starts riding off, but they don't go too fast, so you walks behind. Sometimes along comes another Yank on horse, and he ask, "Boy, ain't you tired?"

"Yes, sir, boss!"

"Well, then, you get up here behind me and ride some." Then he wraps the rope all round the saddle horn. Wraps and wraps but leaves some slack. But he keeps you tied so's you won't jump down and run away. And many's the time a praying Negro got took off like that and wasn't never seen no more.

My marster's name was George Hopper. That man paid taxes on more than two thousand acres of land in two counties. I lived in them two counties in Georgia. My marster never did marry. Lots of folks didn't; they just took up with one another. Marster Hopper had five chillun by my grandmother. She was his house woman; that's what he called her. And when he died, he willed her and all them chillun a house, some land, and a little money. He'd have left them a heap more money and would have been one of the richest men in the county if the war hadn't broke out. When it was over, he had a barrelful of Confederate greenbacks, but it wasn't no-'count. He done broke then.

Talk 'bout hard times! We seed them in those days, during the war and most 'specially after the surrender. Folks these days don't know what trouble looks like. We was glad to eat ashcakes and drink parched corn and rye instead of coffee. I've seed my grandmother go to the smokehouse and scrape up the dirt where the meat had dropped and take it to the house for seasoning. You see, both armies fed off the white folks, and they cleaned out the barns and cellars and smokehouses when they came. And then come the Rebels. When they come, we had 5,000 bushels of corn, 100 head of hogs, 350 gallons of syrup, and such. When they left, they took and set fire to everything to keep it 'way from the Yanks, aiming to starve them out of that country. That's what they done. Some of them Rebs was mean as the Yanks. And that was being mean. Some called the Yanks "the Hornets" 'cause they fight so. Take a Yank, and he'd fight across a buzz saw, and it circling 50 mile a minute.

How come I live in Knoxville? I was a young man when

I started off from Georgia, aiming to go over the mountains to Kentucky, where I heard they pay good wages. I stopped in Campbell County, Tennessee, with another fellow, and I seed a pretty girl working in the field. And I says, "I'm going to marry that gal." Sho' 'nough, me and her was married in less than six months. Her marster built a log house, and we lived there 'til we come to Knoxville.

Now all my boys is dead. Every one worked for Mr. Peters at Peters and Bradley Flour Mills. They all died working for him. So Mr. Willie, he say he going to let me live here in the company house the rest of my days.

I just lay down on that bed nights and watch them automobiles flying by. I say to myself, "Watch them fools!" Folks ain't got the sense they was born with. And times ain't good like they was. If'n it hadn't been for some them crazy fools acting up and smarty, me and my wife would be getting maybe a hundred and more dollars a month, instead of the fifteen we get between us for old-age help. They'd ought to let Roosevelt alone. And it's his own folks is fighting him. He is a big man, even if he is a Democrat. I'm a Republican, though. Voted my first time for [James G.] Blaine [in the 1884 presidential election].

Before I got sick, I would ride the streetcar to town. I goes down to the courthouse, and when I see them cannons in the yard I can't keep from crying. My wife asks me what makes me go look at them cannons if they make me cry. And I tells her I cry 'bout the good and the bad times them cannons bringed on. But no cannons or nothing else seems like going to bring back the good old times. But I don't worry 'bout all these things much. According to the Good Book's promise, “Weeping may endure for a night, then joy come in the morning.” And I know that the day’s soon come when I goes to meet my folks and my Lord and marster in His Heaven, where they ain’t no more weeping.

# They Tried to Make Me Think I Wasn't Free

*I* was born in Mississippi, in Juniper County. I was raised right here in Tennessee 'til I was eleven years old. If I live to see this coming March, I'll be eighty-nine years old. I can't see and hear so well now.

We was raised up without a mother, and one old woman in the house where we stayed was so mean to us she would take nettle weeds and whip us with them.

I had to get up and go to the spring and get water and come back and take breakfast, and my brother Charlie was sick, and we took him out in the yard and let him set up so he could see us play. And after a little while, he said, "I want to lay down. I'm tired of setting up." And I took him and laid him down, and just then they called me to the house to get some eggs to make egg bread. And after I got 'em, I slipped back down to see how he was, and I called him, and he wouldn't answer, and I pulled his eyes open, and he didn't say nothing. And I flew up to the kitchen to Aunt Bet and told her, "Aunt Bet, Charlie's gone to sleep, and I can't wake him up." She went over, and he was dead.

Charlotte—the old woman we was living with—was mean to us. She would make the little one get up and go outdoors to do his business, and he would stay out there 'til I'd come and get him and bring him his breakfast. I would dip my hand in the gravy and rub it on his toes when his feet was cold. And one morning, I brought his breakfast and he couldn't eat, and I tried to open his mouth and I couldn't, so I took him to Aunt Bet. She was my friend. And I said, "Tobe can't eat, and he can't open his mouth." And she come back with me, and Tobe was sitting there and had lockjaw. So she had to go to the white folks, and they sent for the doctor, but he couldn't do no good. And he stayed all that day, but the next night he died. They made me go to the spring and get some water to bathe that child, and it was so dark I couldn't see my hand before my face. And when I got back with the water, Tobe was dead. So I didn't get to see neither one of my brothers die.

When I was eleven, Major Ellison bought me and carried me to Mississippi. I didn't want to go. They examine you just like they do a horse. They look at your teeth and pull your eyelids back and look at your eyes and feel you just like you was a horse. He examined me and said, "Where's your mother?"

And I said, "I don't know where my mammy is, but I know her."

He said, "Would you know your mammy if you saw her?"

And I said, "Yes, sir, I would know her. I don't know where she is, but I would know her." They had done sold her then.

He said, "Do you want us to buy you?"

And I said, "No, I don't want you to buy me. I want to stay here."

He said, "We'll be nice to you and give you plenty to eat."

I said, "No, you won't have much to eat. What do you have to eat?"

And he said, "Lots of peas and cottonseed [probably cottonseed cake, used chiefly as cattle feed] and things like that."

But I said, "No, I'd rather stay here because I get plenty of potlikker and bread and buttermilk, and I don't want to go. I got plenty." I didn't know that that wasn't lots to eat.

He said, "Well, I have married your young mistress, and she wants me to buy you."

But I still said, "I don't want to go." They had done sold my mother to Mr. Armstrong then.

So he kept talking to me, and he said, "Don't you want to see your sister?"

I said, "Yes, but I don't want to go there to see her." They had sold her to Mississippi before that, and I knowed she was there, but I didn't want to go.

I went on back home, and the next day the old white woman whipped me, and I said to myself, "I wish that old white man had bought me." I didn't know he had bought me anyhow.

But soon they took my cotton dresses and put 'em in a

box, and they combed my hair. I heard them tell me that Mr. Ellison had done come after me, and he was in a buggy. I wanted to ride in the buggy, but I didn't want to go with him, so when I saw him I had a bucket of water on my head, and I set it on the shelf and ran just as fast as I could for the woods. They caught me, and Aunt Bet said, "Honey, don't do that. Mr. Ellison done bought you, and you must go with him." She tied my clothes up in a bundle, and he had me sitting up in the buggy with him, and we started to his house here. He was scared I would run away because I had done run away that morning, but I wasn't going to run away 'cause I wouldn't know which way to go after I got that far away.

When we got to the house, my mistress came out with a baby in her arms and said, "Well, here's my little nigger. Shake hands with me."

Then he come up and said, "Speak to your young mistress."

And I said, "Where she at?"

He said, "Right there," and pointed to the baby in my mistress' arms.

I said, "No, I don't see no young mistress. That's a baby."

I went in the house, and they had all the glasses [mirrors] around there, and I just turned and looked and looked at myself, 'cause I had never seen myself in a glass before. I heard Mistress say, "Po' little thing, she's just like a little motherless child. Her mother was sold away from her when she was six years old."

They had soft carpets, and I was just stepping and stamping up and down with my foot 'cause it was so soft. And then she took me up to a big room, and I said to myself,

"Lord God, I got into another fine place!"

The woman in there went in the trunk and got some domestic [cotton fabric] and some calico and made me a dress and some drawers and a drawer body. And she said, "Take them duds and give them to your sister, and you comb her head and wash her all over." And honey, she washed me all over and put them things on me, and I was never dressed so fine in my life, and I just thought everybody was looking at me because I was dressed so fine. But of course, they wasn't paying me no mind at all. The dress had some red in it and some big flowers in it, and I was looking at myself in the glass, and I would pull up my dress and look at my pretty, clean drawers and things. And when I went in the room where my mistress was, I pulled it up again and started looking and saying to myself, "Don't I look nice and clean under here."

And my mistress said, "You mustn't do that. That's ugly."

So then I went out in the woods where there was lots of cedars thick around, and I got down there and pulled up my dress and just looked and danced and danced.

I had never been clean like that before. And staying with them po' white folks, I had had a time with those body lice. They would get so bad I would take my dress off and rub it in the suds and rinse it out in the branch. And sometimes I would be rinsing it and Mistress would call me, and I would be so scared I would put it on wet and run to her. I had a time, I tell you. They might nigh eat me up when I was staying there, and I was so glad to be clean.

The overseer had a bullwhip, and old Marster had a strap,

and I would hear them out in the field beating them, and the slaves would just be crying, "Oh, pray, Marster. Oh, pray, Marster."

Ole Miss wouldn't let 'em whip me. She was just like a mammy to me. I wanted to die, too, when she died. Yes, she died right here in town. She called me in and told me, "Lu, I'm dying, but you be good to my chillun." And Marse Tom would fan her, but she would always say, "Give it to Lu. You fan too hard, and I don't want you fanning the breath out of me. It's going fast enough without you fanning it away." I stood there and fanned her 'til she breathed her last, and then I ran in the next room and hugged my arms right around me and hold my breath and tried my best to die. I was scared of Mr. Ellison 'cause he cussed so much.

I used to make the chillun cry during the war. I would say, "I'm going to the Yankees. Miss Maggie's getting just so mean to me."

And the youngest child would say, "We'll go, too. I'll tell you which-a-way to go." And she woulda went with me, too. All of them chillun woulda went if I'd run away then. I had a hard time, I tell you.

When the war was coming up, I would hear the white folks reading the papers about it, and I would run in the kitchen and tell Aunt Harriet. She would say, "Don't let the white folks hear you talk. They'll kill you." And if I would be going too far, she would stop me and wouldn't let me finish telling it to her.

I married 'rectly after the war ceasted. My old boss married his own niggers in Mississippi. He'd just get the Bible and marry them, and he had the 'surance [assurance] to marry me after the war, and he had to pay ten dollars for it, too, 'cause he wasn't no officer that could marry me.

I come up here [Nashville] the first year of the war, and I never did get back. I stayed with my white folks three years after Freedom, and they tried to make me think I wasn't free.

One Sunday, I wanted to go to a meeting in Franklin, and I didn't ask. I just told this woman I was going, and she said, "I say you can't go."

And I said, "Oh, yes, I'm going."

And she called Marse Tom, and I told him I was going, and he said, "I say you can't go."

So I said, "You look right here, Marse Tom. I'm free, just as free as the birds in the air. You didn't tell me, but I know it."

And he didn't say another word. You see, they thought that 'cause I stayed there I was fool enough not to know I was free. But I knowed it. And I went on to Franklin. I was nine miles from town, but I walked there to the meeting.

Later on, they wanted me to go down to Mississippi to live, but I said, "I never 'spect to go to old 'Sip' again, long as I live." The chillun kissed me and told me good-bye, and they cried and cried.

Later on, he bought here, and they moved back, and I would go up there every month to see how my chillun was getting along. They would meet me down at a big tree and tell me, "She [the children's stepmother] is just as mean to us as she can be." And they would take me up to the house and give me lots of things to carry home with me. I would tell Marse Tom I come after some money and some clothes, too, and he'd give me a dollar and tell them to give me what I wanted, and they would go to the smokehouse and give me some meat and anything else I wanted. I still can get anything I want if I go to them, but it is hard for me to get way up there now.

My daughter is just fifteen years younger'n I am. Her daddy died during the war.

I don't know nothing about my mother and father. She left us and run off, and I was the oldest, and she left me and a little brother and another little suckling baby. She took us to the back porch at Morrison's and left us. I remember that Morrison come out of the door, and he asked me what we was doing there, and I told him Mammy told us to stay there 'til she got back. And he asked where she went, and I told him I didn't know. He went back and said to his wife, "Fannie, Ada's done run away, and her chillun's out on the front porch." Then he come back and told me to take the baby and my little brother and go round to the kitchen.

Mama, she run away, and she stayed right here in town with ole Carter for about a year, and after she'd paid him fifty dollars to keep him from telling on her, he 'trayed her. So she found it out, and she left the barn where she was staying and come on back home. She seen ole Carter pointing out the barn to a nigger trader, and she left there. Ole Morrison kept her about two weeks after she come back, and a nigger trader come along, and he sold her. He said it was no good for him to keep her, 'cause if he'd hire her out she would whip the white folks. She had a scar right up over her eye, and she got it fighting white folks. I remember it 'cause I remember getting slapped about picking at it when I was little.

When she come back after Freedom, she was here in town a week before I knowed it. I had just had a fight with my husband, and I had just told him that if I had a mammy to go to I would leave and never come back to him. That night, we had gone to bed, and it was raining real hard, and I heard somebody holler, and I thought it was somebody coming for him to hunt. He said they could just holler on then. And that was my mother and my little half-brother then. It was dark, and they was at the river, and they couldn't find the foot log. So they finally found somebody and asked them how far it was to Mr. Mayberry's place, and they told her to turn around and walk three miles back down the pike. And when she got there, they told her it was back the way she come, and to go to some of the colored folks' house and stay 'til morning and get an early start. So she went and knocked on a door, but just as soon as she did they put all the lights out, and nobody wouldn't come to the door. So she went back to the white man's barn and got in the hay and stayed all night, and in the morning she got up and come walking up to my house in the rain. It was in February. She walked up to the door and asked who lived here. I told her Kay Mayberry lived here, and I'm his wife. So she said, "You don't know me?"

And I said, "No'm, I don't believe I made your acquaintance before, but come in out of the rain."

And she come in and asked me again if I knowed her, and she stepped over to the door. But I didn't know her, and the boy said, "This is your mother, and I'm your brother."

I said, "No, my mother's sold, and my brothers are dead." And I said, "You're none of my mammy; I know my mammy." Then she took the bundle off her head and took off her hat, and I saw that scar on her face. Child, look like I had wings! I hollered for everybody. I 'larmed out all the neighbors.

She stayed with us a long time, and she died right here in this house.

# They Would Turn a Kettle Upside Down

Ellis Ken Kannon

I don't know jest how old I is. I was born in Tennessee as a slave. My mammy come from Virginia. Our marster was Ken Kannon.

Our mistress wouldn't let us slaves be whipped, but I remember my daddy telling about the overseer whipping him, and he run away and hid in a log. He heard the bloodhounds about a mile away on his trail, could hear him breathe, but the hounds never found him. After the hounds passed on, my daddy left the log hiding place, and when he got to a blacksmith shop he seed a white man with a nigger who had handcuffs on. And when the white man took off the handcuffs, the nigger asked my daddy where he was going, and he told them, "Back to my mistress"

And the nigger says, “I is, too.”

My daddy slipped away from him and went home.

When I was a young boy, I didn’t wear nothing but a shirt like all other boys, and it was a long thing like a slip that come to our knees. Our mistress had a big fireplace, and when we would come in cold she would say, “Ain’t you-all cold?” While we was warming, she often played the organ for us to hear.

I waited on my marster ’til he died. They let me stay right with the body. My mistress, mammy of the marster, was in bad health at that time. ’Fore we started for the graveyard, I put a feather bed in the carriage and got a pitcher of water ready, and ’fore we get there she got awful sick.

During slavery, the slaves had to keep quiet, and they would turn a kettle upside down to keep the white folks [from] hearing their prayers and chants.

When a slave wanted to go to another plantation, he had to have a pass. If he disobeyed, he got a whipping. And if they had a pass without the marster’s signature, they got a whipping. If’n they had to have passes now, there wouldn’t be no meanness.

I remember the Ku Klux Klan coming to my daddy’s home asking for water, and they would keep us toting water to them for fifteen to twenty minutes. They didn’t whip or hurt any of us. I also remember my mammy and daddy telling us ’bout the stars falling. I remember the comet. It was a big ball and had a long tail.

I have heard them tell ’bout Mr. Robertson. He was mean to his slaves, and they says they could see a ball of fire rolling on the fence, and when they would get to the spring a big white thing like a dog would crawl under the rock. The slaves was naturally superstitious and believed in dreams, old sayings, and signs. I have myself seen things that I ain't understand.

After Freedom, most of the slaves worked for their living, just as I said, the men in the fields, the women in the house. I worked at a hotel in McMinnville, and one day I was keeping the flies off the table with a brush made from fine strips of paper, and the string broke, and it fell on the table. One man jumped up, grabbed a chair, saying, "I'll knock you down with this chair."

The slaves expected to get forty acres of land and a mule, but nobody ever got it, as far as I know. He didn't get nothing. Our white people wasn't able to give us anything. Everything they had was taken during the war. They was good to us and stuck with us, and my people stayed with my mistress.

This young generation of niggers, I declare, they is just about gone. They won't work. All's stealing, and maybe work long enough to get a few clothes to strut around in. I may be wrong, but that is my honest opinion.

I has been here fifteen years and have worked under two priests and now working under the third. They have all been nice to me. Have never had any trouble with white people, and you'd be surprised how good they is to me. They don't treat me like a nigger.

Ever since I got Freedom and 'fore I got this church job, I done all kinds of odd jobs—waited on tables, pressing clothes, and anything else that come along. Some jobs was small pay but kept me alive.

# They Charged Him for His Own Child

Susanna

(last name unknown)

In those days, when my mother was coming up, white folks kept their [slaves'] ages, and the colored folks didn't even know. You know, even when they got ready to marry, it was the white folks that give them permission.

I came from Virginia. They called it "old Virginny" then, you know. When white folks got a notion to move to Tennessee or anywhere, they just taken the colored folks up, and course my grandmother had to go, too. They traveled in wagons in those days, but my grandmother don't remember nothing about her parents. The biggest thing I remember about my grandmother was that she was foolish about her hair. It was black as satin, and she was what they called Cold Creek Indian.

Well, they brought her from old Virginny to Tennessee when she was but a child; they settled in Gallatin. It is a big, flourishing town now. While she was there, there came another family named Alaskas; this was Grandpap's family. Now, Grandma's folks was named Perry. You see, Grandma was their house girl, and Grandpap was Alaskas' houseboy. They kept her because she was young and supple and could have lots of children. Ain't that hard? She waited on the missus and did the little, nice things about the house, you know. You see, their object was to raise her and sell her so she would make a lot of money for them.

Well, Grandpap was young and just as black as satin and real handsome, and Grandma was getting to the age where she liked young men. They begin courting. I asked Grandma why she wanted to fool with him, and she say he was nice and handsome and a right likely young man, you know. Well, they kept on courting back and forth, and finally she married him. And you know, when she married him, he didn't have on nothing but a shirt; that's all they give them to wear then. Grandma wore a long cotton dress, sometimes no stockings and shoes; that's all they had to wear. Ain't that hard?

When they went to camp meetings or to church, Grandma rode up behind her white folks, and Grandpap rode up behind his'n. They went to preaching every Sunday, and Grandma said the preacher would say, "Servants, obey your master," every Sunday. And you know, they thought that he was talking about the earthly master, and the white folks didn't want them to know no better. Grandma said they would feed you well, but they didn't enlighten you none nor let you have no books to learn from. Ain't that hard?

They spun our clothes. You see, they was thrifty. And the shoes was nothing but treated goat hide, all rough on the inside.

Well, as I said, Grandma got attached to Grandpap. She thought he was the prettiest man she ever saw. They kept courting, and finally the two families decided one to buy the other. That is, either the Alaskas was to buy Grandpap or the Perrys buy Grandma. Grandpap's people was a little bit better off than Grandma's, so they bought Grandma. Guess what they charged for her? They charged a hundred dollars for every year that she was old. Yes, sir, that's what they charged for her. Ain't that awful? They called that marrying them.

Well, after so long a time, my mother was born. Grandpap's white folks claimed Mother. But Grandpap was smart; he wanted to come out of the woods. If you was smart enough to buy yourself, you could become a freeman, but then you had to mingle with the free folks. That is, you couldn't have nothing to do with slaves, 'cause you might fool them off, too, you see. So if the white folks would consent to let you buy yourself, you could become free.

Well, Grandpap decided to buy himself, and so he told the white folks. He come up to Nashville and hired out in a hotel called the Nashville Inn. He was what they called a bedroom servant. You see, the white folks—that is, his white folks—hired him to the Nashville Inn so he would pay for himself, do you understand? They needed the money, so they told him, "Well, Hardy, we need money, so we'll let you pay for yourself, and you can be free." Now, every Saturday, he would make about five or ten dollars that he would give to them. Now, you see, that was just like a hundred dollars now. He didn't have no expenses 'cause he had plenty to eat and somewhere to sleep.

Well, he worked and worked 'til I guess he paid them about eight hundred dollars in all for himself. Then one day, they sent for him, and they said, "Well, Hardy, you are a freeman. You can go anywhere you please, but you can't take Catherine." Well, he was just like any other man—he wanted Catherine with him. So he turned round, and the white folks made him pay the same for Grandma. He worked and worked some more, and he finally paid for her. Then they come to town, and they still worked in this Nashville Inn. Grandma, she washed the fine linens and let that money go on her Freedom.

Well, you see, they had bought themselves, but they had left my mother, three years old, up in Gallatin. Grandma said she cried and worried over her all the time. She was crazy about her child, and it was pitiful to hear her tell about how she worried about her. Then they put after old Missus to know what she would ask for my mother. Old Missus said, "Catherine is a likely child, and we will take care of her 'til she gets older, and then we can sell her for a lot of money." Well, they kept after the white folks 'til finally they charged him for his own child. They charged him $350. Just think of that. You see, she was 'bout three and a half years old, and they charged him $100 a year. Ain't that awful?

Well, they bought her. And you see, there was the three of 'em. Well, the white folks gave them a paper signed by them, and they could go anywhere in Tennessee they wanted to, but they wouldn't be free out of the state, you see. They was already here in Nashville, you know. Well, has you ever been on the square, up here at the marketplace? Right on this side of the square is where I was born, in that brick house where they is an old paint factory right now. They named me Susanna; I was born in 1858, along in May. Miss Lizzie Elliott—you oughta know her—well, anyway, she remembers that I was born about that time. I was awful smart and used to run and take messages and do errands for folks; I liked to do errands for folks.

My grandmother had another boy and another girl, but my mother was the oldest child, and she married a man named Martin Howard. He was a candle maker. You know, they used to have these old candle makers, made good money in them days. Well, after I was born, my mother and father decided they was going to get something for themselves. They said, "Now, we been working for the white folks all the time, and we got a little saved up, so we going to make something for our children." So they got to work, and he opened up a carriage place. He ran that place for forty years, right up there on the square. Him and Grandpap had four hacks, three express wagons—carryalls, they called them then—two drays, and about eight horses. That is what Grandpap left her when he died. The old brick building is there today. He run that trade for years. Everybody knew him.

Well, my mother, she married by consent, just like her mother and father did. But Mother was free, but the white folks had to get permission from old man Howard to marry her. He's the same Howard that gave the Congregational church over here on Twelfth Avenue to the colored folks. He was Pap's master, you know. Old Howard was James D.

Porter's brother-in-law. You know Governor Porter; he served three terms 'cause he was such a good white man. I used to have an old trunk with all the announcements and everything in them, but you know how things like that get away.

Way back in them days, people would have no doctors like they do now. They would go out and got wild sage. Yes'm, they used that for stomachache, and they would get some dog fennel and make a real splendid tea. 'Nother thing they used to have was slippery elm tea, and they would put it in a little crock pitcher and jest set it aside and drink out of it when they got ready. Most of the times, they would give tansy tea to little babies and children for the colic. Then sometimes girls your size, you know, took this tansy tea. We used to use the old-fashioned quinine and asafiddy [asafetida] for colds and such-like ailments. You know, tumors wasn't common like they is now. It was a rare thing to hear of the TB, too.

I know you going to laugh when you hear this. You sho' won't believe this. But you know, they used to wear pettiskirts, they called them then. And my mother used to quilt my skirts from way up here round the thigh down to the bottom. Yes, sirree, I know it's funny now. But one thing, you never could take no cold with that nice warm quilted skirt on, and long underwear and an old-fashioned lined dress skirt.

The po' white folks couldn't even come on our place. They tried to get the best white man among the po' trash for overseer. Most of the refined white folks wouldn't want the overseer to whip the niggers. They rather for them to be properly fed, and then they could work best, just like cattle.

My father's white folks would not have a po' white man on the place.

That's the trouble with our folks. They is still jealous of the po' white man. Since colored people have got free, they is taking the white folks' jobs, and the white folks don't like it. They the one what ought to be jealous. And they is 'fraid if the colored girl come out in her straight hair and high-heeled shoes and neat dress, they will get their jobs.

# I Was Sold Away from My Husband

## Millie Simpkins

*I* claims I's 109 years old and was born near Winchester, Tennessee. My marster was Boyd Sims, and my missus was Sarah Ann Ewing Sims. My mammy was named Judy Ewing, and my daddy was Moses Stephens, and he was freeborn. He was the marster's stableboy and followed the races. He run away and never came back.

My first missus was very rich. She had two slaves come to dress her every morning, and I brought her breakfast to her on a silver waiter. She was married three times. Her second husband was Joe Carter, and the third was Judge Gork.

My first missus sold me 'cause I was stubborn. She sent me to the slave yard at Nashville. The yard was full of slaves. I stayed there two weeks 'fore Marster Simpkins bought me.

I was sold away from my husband, and I never seed him again. I had one chile, which I took with me.

The slave yard was on Cedar Street. A Mr. Chandler would bid the slaves off, but 'fore they started bidding, you had to take all of your clothes off and roll down the hill, so they could see that you didn't have no bones broken or sores on you. I wouldn't take mine off. If nobody bid on you, you was took to the slave mart and sold. I was sold there. A bunch of them was sent to Mississippi, and they had their ankles fastened together, and they had to walk while the traders rode.

When I was sold to Marster Simpkins, my second mistress made me a house slave, and I worked only at the big house. My work was to nurse and dress the chillun and help my missus in her dressing. The young slaves was hired out to nurse the white chillun. I was hired as a nurse girl at seven years old and started cooking at ten. I never had a chance to go to school.

I'm the mammy of fourteen chillun, seven boys and seven gals. I was next to the oldest of four chillun. My missus used to hire me out to hotels and taverns.

Some marsters fed their slaves mean, and some wouldn't let them have a bite. One marster we used to hear about would grease his slaves' mouths on Sunday morning and tell them if anybody asked if they had meat to say, "Yes, lots of it."

When they got ready to whip them, they'd put them down on a pit without any clothes, stand back with a bullwhip, and cut the blood out. I remember the niggers would run away and hide out.

The only fun the young folks had was when the old folks had a quilting. While the old folks was working on the quilt, the young ones would get in another room, dance, and have a good time. They's have a pot turned down at the door to keep the white folks from hearing them.

The white folks didn't want us to learn nothing, and if a slave picked up a little piece of paper they would yell, "Put that down, you! You want to get in our business."

The white folks wouldn't let the slaves pray. If they got to pray, it was while walking behind the plow. White folks would whip the slaves if they heard them sing or pray.

I was a big girl when they built the capitol. I played on the hill 'fore it was built, and I tote blocks from there when it was being built.

I was living in Dickson County when Fort Donelson was took. I seed the first gunboat that come up the Cumberland River. I was standing in the door when I seed it coming, but it didn't take me long to get back in the back of the house. I was scared they would shoot. My marster ran a ferry, and after the gunboat come up the river he got scared and give my old man the ferry. And when the soldiers come to take Fort Negley, he set them across the river. I was right here when the Civil War was going on, and the soldiers was dressed up and beating the drums.

No, honey, we didn't get nothing when we was freed. Just drove away without nothing to do with. We got in a wagon and drove to another man's plantation. Some of the slaves might have got something, but I don't know nobody that did.

I was scared to open my door after dark on account of

the Ku Klux Klan. They was red-hot.

I's cooked ever since I was freed. I stayed in Henry Gable's kitchen five long years, and since I's had these strokes, it's broke me up 'til I can do nothing. I belong to the Methodist Church. I think these young people is terrible, and this white-and-black marriage not be 'lowed.

I was here when Henry Clay and James K. Polk was running. I was hired at the old City Hotel over on the river. I was a dining-room servant there. My marster would have me sing a song for him 'bout the Democrats:

> "Hooray, the country is rising;
> Rise up and drown old Clay in his pizen."

I guess old Clay was a right good fellow, but he played cards with the niggers in the cellar.

I always stay with my daughter. That is the only support I have since I had these strokes and been unable to do for myself.

# I Stole My Learning in the Woods

*I* am about eighty-five years old. I wasn't old enough to go to the Civil War, but I was such a big boy they thought I was old enough to go. I was playing marbles when they took me to the war. I was born in Henry County, near Paris, Tennessee, and been round 'bout there most of my life.

I remember before they carried me off we was down on the ground playing marbles, and we saw some soldiers coming, and we started running, and they caught us and wanted to know what we was running for, and I told them we was running from the Lincolnites. He said they wasn't gonna hurt us. It was right funny. I was talking to a Lincolnite and didn't know it.

I could hear the colored people talk about they was gonna

be free, but I didn't have sense to know what they was talking about. It wasn't any way for the colored people to get away, for they always had bloodhounds to catch you if you started running away.

We played marbles then, just about like the boys do now, only we had four square rings, and I think they have diamonds now. We played Molly Bright and Three Score and Ten.

My mother stayed in the house all the time. I never knowed her to get out of my sight. My mother had twelve children, four boys and eight girls. She was a cook. Her owner set them at liberty about three years before the Civil War and give them a home as long as they lived. They had worked her enough, I reckon. Before her mistress died, she liberated all of her people. She never did sell none of Mother's children from her. Her son was a lawyer in that town. My father was foreman over all her slaves. We had pretty good treatment.

When they carried me away, they fooled me on the horse. I didn't know nothing 'bout where I was going, for I was nothing but a boy. They carried me off somewhere near Nashville. I was there about two years.

I remember once Mistress had a big red apple setting on her table, and I had planned to steal it. I bit down in it, and it wasn't nothing but soap. That was a good one on me. They let us go to the table to eat after they got through eating. They raised all kinds of vegetables. She had a fine carriage, and she went to Memphis every fall.

I have seen colored people treated all kinds of ways in my life. I have seen them beat 'til the blood run out of them.

I could do any kind of plowing. I worked in the field. And at night, we used to play marbles in the house. We would make a ring on the floor by candlelight. Sometimes they would wait 'til you was ten years old before they put you to plowing. I used to chop with the hoe, and plow. I would get a nice little whipping sometimes when trying to plow, 'cause I wouldn't do it right. They had a great deal of hogs. They used to send me to feed the hogs and horses.

I never went to but one wedding while I was little. I slipped off and went to that one. My father whipped the fire out of me, too. The preacher said some kind of ceremony out of the Bible, but they didn't have no license.

Boys wasn't like these now. We didn't pay no 'tention to people courting. We had a little trundle bed, and when we was put in it we didn't see no more 'til the next morning, and we had better keep quiet, too. We never did see daylight after we was put in that bed until the next morning. Their beds was high enough to roll ours under theirs. They had hemp rope across their bed to keep from falling in on us.

Our white folks was pretty good to us. They would let the slaves have a garden, and let one build a little chicken house and sell chickens. He had more chickens than the white folks did. Some of the slaves would go away up to Canada, where there was some free slaves.

Colored people didn't get sick and die like they do now. They had little things but not serious diseases. I don't know why, but they just didn't do it.

Mistress was a mighty church member. They told me mostly what I know. When her husband died, they bought twelve candles and burnt six of them and kept the other six until she died. The colored people used the white folks' church after they preaching was over.

The ladies all wore long skirts and used bamboo briars to make them tilt. When boys got pretty large, they wore body breeches. They wore a shirt and nothing else until they got a certain age. They wore something kinda like these coveralls they wear now.

Old lady used to make that old-fashioned hominy so many times a week. She had one of these cockleshells just like a snail shell that she blowed for the hands to come to dinner. I kept it a long time after she died. Old man Peter blowed his first; he was the kind of leader in blowing. And my mother would blow hers then. The white folks would eat in the dining room, and the hands would eat in the kitchen.

I think they treated the house slaves a little better than they did the others. Some of them was bright, and some was brown skin. My sister said that my old mistress's father was my mother's father. The children take some after him in color, and some after her. Speculators used to come round every week after slaves, but they didn't never sell none of them.

I stole my learning in the woods. When I was a little boy, I always wanted to know what was on a piece of paper. I got a spelling book, and in the night I would try to got my lessons. One night, I was down on the floor trying to spell when Marster come in and asked me what I was doing, and I told him I was trying to spell. He made me spell *farm* and told me that he didn't want to catch me spelling no more. After that, I had to steal what little learning I had.

I had a brother who got to the line of Canada. We all had Freedom in our bones. "Give me liberty or give me death" was in my bones. I read that since Freedom. Patrick Henry said that.

I had a brother-in-law who was going to buy my oldest sister for nine hundred dollars, but Freedom come just about the time he was going to buy her. He was a barber. There was a right smart free folks around here. Jane Randall and her three daughters and one son was free. I knowed a man named Wyatt who was free, and he wanted to marry a slave girl name Carrie, and he gave himself to Carrie's master, to marry her. That love is an awful thing, I tell you. I don't think I would give my Freedom away to marry anybody. What I woulda done was to go off and send for her later on. He was crazy to do that. They treated the free colored people pretty rough. But after all, they had better privileges than a slave, if they didn't go crazy about some slave girl and give hisself away.

I didn't know I was a slave until once they cut darkies' heads off in a riot. They put their faces up like a sign-board. They said they was going to burn niggers up by the hundreds.

I have heard a heap of people say they wouldn't take the treatment what the slaves took, but they woulda took it or death. If they had been there, they woulda took the very same treatment.

Say, is there any danger in this talk? If so, I want to take back everything I said.

# They Sold My Sister Right in This Nigger-Trading Yard

Name unknown

We were set free in 1865. I was grown and old enough to be married. Girls didn't marry so fast in those days. They says now they want to have a booth for another colored woman and myself in the World's Fair.

The thirteenth of this last March, I entered into my ninetieth year. I was born in 1842 at Elkton, Todd County, Kentucky. At that time, the Yankee teachers were just beginning to come south, and my mother was a cook at the academy there, and I was born there. Mr. and Mrs. Dickey taught the boys and girls there. My sister was a nurse there at the time—my oldest sister. This lady taught my sister how to read and write, unbeknowingst to the white people. They didn't allow it.

After we were set free, my sister taught here in Tennessee. Her name was Sally Johnson. They taught school right over on that hill. She taught the first free school that was here in Clarksville after the Yankees left. At that time, we belonged to the Hudsons. My first people was from Culpeper, Virginia—big families, white and colored, and all dead but me and my son. I never left Kentucky until after we were set free over here in Christian County. I crossed over here after Christmas and went to school to a Yankee teacher named Kenny. Him and his son taught a school.

My mistress and master had over seventy-five slaves. I cut and sewed for them two years before I was set free. I sewed on the first sewing machine that ever come south. I can cut and sew yet. They dressed me awful nice and treated us all nice. If everybody would work, times wouldn't be like they is. Too many people won't work.

My young master married a Miss Nannie Long, and then he give me to her for a maid. They taken me from mother on Christmas, and I was not six years old until March. I never lived with my mother; I lived right in the house with the white folks. I carried a white child on my arm most of the time. Of course, I had company, but at nine o'clock I had to go into the house. I was never treated mean.

Yes, I went to parties and danced all night on Saturday night, dressed to death. I used to go to parties, and they all treated me nice. I never had a young man, white or colored, to say an ugly word to me, because my young master was very strict with me. Girls don't have to mind nowadays like they used to.

My father was white, a Quaker. He wanted to buy me

when I was old enough to be taken from my mother, so I could be raised in Philadelphia. His name was Dick Black. But they wouldn't sell me. He owned a store.

When I came to Clarksville, all over there was woods. There was a big spring, and all of us used to go down there to get water. That was after we was set free. All this place has been cleared off. I been here a long time, and I ain't tired of staying.

My mother had eight children. All of them were not my father's children. I was the only one by him. Mother married, and her husband's master used to run what was called stages, before trains ever come out. The stage would come from Elkton to Russellville and from Russellville to Hopkinsville. And when the trains began coming south, his master moved where he could still run his stage. That separated them, but she never did marry again. Don't know so much about Grandmother—my mother's mother. Aunt Jane would have been over a hundred years old. She nursed Mother's children, and then she nursed Robert, my son, until he was eight years old, when she died. I buried her and Mother in Louisville. Mother lived to be over seventy-four. My mother was your color; she was dark.

My brother and his wife were thirty-three-degree Masons; Brother Joe died in Hickman, Kentucky. I had no whole brothers and sisters—all halves. And nobody living but me and my boy; even the white people are all dead.

My sister was brought here from Elkton. And there used to be a nigger-trading place right here where the Clarksville National Bank is, right on that place. They sold my sister right in this nigger-trading yard. She had a baby, and at first they didn't want to buy her because of the baby, but finally a man from Arkansas bought them, and my mother never heard nothing of her for twelve years.

Before we were set free, there come a gypsy down through Kentucky, telling fortunes. The white people didn't allow them to come in the front door. So them took them around to the kitchen. While one of them was there, she looked at Mother and said, "I think I can tell you something that you might like to hear." And she said, "Your daughter who you haven't seen or heard from for twelve years is living and doing well, but she has got six other children." That made seven. She told Mother all about how well she was living. She said, "Why, she goes to the springs every summer with these children, and has two nurses."

During slavery, we had to work. Mr. Crab was a mighty good man. His father bought a farm and put them on it and had these slaves. He was a good man, but everybody had to work. That's what got the country in this condition; people don't want to work. He was very good to his slaves. Of course, I didn't have anything to do with them. It is just like, you come here and buys three of us and put a man or woman over us. He was paid so much money a year to run the farm, but he didn't have nothing to do with the women of the house or the houseboys. But them on the farm were under the overseer, and if they didn't do their work they got a whipping, a mighty bad whipping. They were mighty mean at that time, some of them. When they commenced running off 'cross the Mason-Dixon line, they would catch them, tie them on a barrel, and whip them to death sometime. They whipped a young man named Montgomery so hard that he didn't have no skin on his back. When they whipped them, they took salt and water and poured it on the backs. They would have you strapped down and whip you from your head down to your feet.

I tell you, daughter, it was mighty hard, and colored people oughtn't be so mean to one another. I always cried every day to see how colored people don't love one another, to see how people have died before they set them free.

I never got but one whipping before I was grown, and that was because I whipped my mistress. What I got this whipping about, the mistress rang the bell, and I didn't come right away, and she asked me why I didn't come, and I told her I come as quick as I could, and she whacked me across the head with a broomstick, and I whacked her back and got a good whipping. When her husband came, he whipped me across my shoulders with a cowhide, and Miss Betty had always whipped me with a switch. But I didn't care then if they had killed me.

That's why so many colored people got killed; they just whipped them for nothing. I had an uncle, my mother's brother. His name was Nelson, and he lived on the Culpeper line. They wanted to whip him, and he didn't let them, and they got another overseer to help them. When they came up to Uncle Nelson, they took him out here near the bluff, right by the river. They said to Uncle Nelson, "We are going to get you."

Uncle Nelson said, "Yes, we will all go to Hell together."

And they both were drowned.

My old mistress thought a lot of me. I was the maid and

had to take care of the mistress's children. She had a lot of money, but she never would put it in the bank. When my old mistress died, she had four children, and her oldest daughter married and gone up north. I never did know my mistress to go away from home. She hid all that money upstairs. There were no banks, and so people had to hide their money. I laugh a heap of times about an old bureau and a little trunk that she had, and I wanted her to let me put my doll clothes in it, but she would say, "Don't touch it." After she died, it was found out that she kept her gold money in it. Then in the bureau, she had kept some money so long that it was as black as your dress, and I thought it was buttons, but when it was rubbed off it was money. She even had money tied up in fringe on her bedspreads.

Mr. Crab kept Joe because he was my mother's youngest child. House slaves and the other slaves got along fine. They all got along nicely. They had what is called nigger quarters. Had a great, long table set three times a day, and two boys waited on it. These quarters were about as far as across the street from the big house. They got hats, shoes, clothes, and bedclothes and were well treated. After they were set free, many of them stayed there until they broke up. They didn't want me to leave because I was her maid, but Sister come after me so I could come over here and go to school. Mother stayed there until after I come here and married. Then her and Joe come here and lived over here on Franklin Street. Colored people had all that street right after the war. Then white people come here and run them out.

We used to have all our dances in the courthouse. My

sister taught school right up here in the college and had 125 scholars. They used to have a song about

> "Old Master's gone away,
> And the darkies stayed at home;
> Must be now that the Kingdom's come
> And the year for Jubilee."

When the war came on, we stayed. [We were] scared—what else could we do? The men had come to Fort Donelson. I stayed hid about three days and nights in a cornfield. They thought that I had come like so many women and girls, to cook at Fort Donelson. Fort Donelson was the biggest place that the colored people had for their quarters, and I been there many times since.

I never seen nobody that I could speak to, for so many people would tell on you then. And they do that today. Colored people has got to be more loving.

I run off and married right over there in the schoolhouse, and then he carried me on out to his house. I had one son, and he is a Revenue man in Chicago. I left the farm when he was four and a half years old. His father just got so mean I couldn't stay with him. I took my son to Louisville, Kentucky, and raised him there.

I have always worked hard. I run a lace laundry yet. I have made as high as eight dollars a day up here at my place on Ninth Street. My son graduated from the grammar school in Louisville and graduated at Fisk. He was old enough to be called in the Spanish-American War and was promoted corporal before he come out of that war. He went from here to Evansville and then on to Chicago, where he worked in the movies. And a fellow got him to try at the post office, and he got on it there and is a Revenue man yet. He sends me a check the fifteenth of every month. He is about sixty-three. My first husband was Robert Outlaw, and now my boy is named Robert Outlaw. He had three children and lost them all. I go to see them every summer and stay awhile.

I have Robert's little bellyband, shoes, underskirt, a dress I paid five dollars for that come from England, a little hat, and I got them all yet. I am going to put them all on [display at] the [World's] Fair and leave them there. Then I got a dress that was made the first year after the Civil War. A lady named Mrs. Pritchard taken the premium in Nashville with that dress. It is made Martha Washington style. I have got a pin that I have had ever since all of Clarksville like to have burned down, and that was in 1872. And it is said that all the fire departments came from Nashville, and only the colored fire department put it out. They were going to hang a man out from here, and while they were all out there a darky set Clarksville on fire, and they ain't never been another attempt at hanging another colored man here since.

# One Night a Ku Klux Klan Rode Up to Our Door

Frankie Goole

*I* was born in Williamson County, on the other side of Lebanon. I'll be eighty-five years old on Christmas Day.

My ole missus was named Sallie, and my marster was George Waters. My mammy's name was Lucindia. She was sold from me when I was six weeks old, and my missus raised me. I always slept with her. My missus was good to me, but her son and my marster whipped me.

I remember the Ku Klux Klan and the patterollers. They would come round and whip the niggers with a bullwhip. If'n they met a nigger on the road, they'd say, "Where is you going this time of mornin'?"

The slaves would say, "We is going over here to stay awhile."

And then they would start beating them.

I've stood in our door and heard the hard licks and screams of the ones that was being whipped, and I'd tell my missus, "Listen to that!"

She would say, "See, that is what will happen to you if you try to leave."

I remember one night a Ku Klux Klan rode up to our door. I told my missus somebody was at the door wanting to know where my marster was. She told them he was dead and her son had gone away that morning. He hunted all through the house and up in the loft and said, "Where is the niggers?" My missus told him they was down in the little house. He went down there, woke them up, asked them about their marster, and then whipped all of them.

If they had the Ku Klux Klan now, there would be so many peoples on the county road and in the pen.

When the niggers was freed, all of my missus' slaves slipped away 'cept me. One morning, she told me to go down and wake them up. I went down and knocked. Nobody said nothin'. I pushed on the door, it come open, and I fell in the room and hurt my chin. I went back to the missus, and she says, "What's the matter with you?"

I says, "Uncle John and all of them is gone. I pushed on the door and fell in."

She says, "You know they is not gone. Go back and get them up." I had to go back, but they weren't there.

My missus didn't give me nothing 'cept my clothes, and she put them in a carpetbag. After Freedom, my mammy come from Lebanon and got me. I'll never forget that day—oh Lawdy! I can see her now. My ole missus' daughter-in-law had got a bunch of switches to whip me. I was standing in the door shaking all over, and the young missus was telling me to get my clothes off. I says, "I seed a woman coming through the gate."

My missus says, "That is Lucindia," and the young missus hid the switches.

My mammy says, "I've come to get my chile."

My missus told her to let me spend the night with her, then she'd send me to the courthouse at nine o'clock the next morning. So I stayed with the missus that night, and she told me to always be a good girl and don't let a man or boy trip me. I didn't know what she mean, but I always remembered what she said. I guess I was about twelve years old when I left my missus, and my mammy brought me to Nashville and put me to work.

The morning I left my missus, I went to the courthouse and met my mammy. The courtroom was jammed with people. The judge told me to hold my right hand up. I was so scared I stuck both hands up. Judge says, "Frankie, is that your mammy?"

I says, "I don't know. She says she is." What did I know of a mammy that was took from me at six weeks old?

He says, "Was your marster good to you?"

I says, "My missus was, but my marster wasn't. He whipped me."

The judge says, "Where did he whip you?" I told him on my back. He says, "Frankie, is you laughing?"

I says, "No, sir."

He said to my mammy, "Lucindia, take this chile and be

good to her, for she has been mistreated. Someday she can make a living for you."

And thank the Lawd, I did keep her in her ole days and was able to bury her. At that time, money was called chin plaster [shinplaster], and when I left out of the courtroom different people give me money, and I had my hat almost full. That was the only money I had give to me.

I nursed Miss Sadie Pope Fall; she married Mat Gardner. I also nursed Miss Sue Porter Houston. I then worked at the blind school.

The first pair of shoes I had was after I come to Nashville. They had high tops and was called booties. I had some red-stripe socks with them.

I went to school one year at Fisk in 1869.

The last man I worked for was at the Link Hotel. Then I started keeping boarders. Have fed all these Nashville police. The police is the ones that helped get relief orders for me. I have lived on this street for sixty years. I lived twenty-two years where the Hermitage Laundry is. That is where I got the name "Mammy." While living there, I raised eighteen chillun, white and black, and some of them is good to me now.

I sometimes wish for the good ole days. These days, folks don't have time for religion. The doggone ole radio and other things taking its place.

Oh Lawdy, how they did baptize down at the wharf. The Baptist people would gather at the wharf on the first Sunday in May. They would come from all the Baptist churches. Would leave the church singing and shouting and keep that up 'til they got to the river. Have seen them with new clothes on get down on the ground and roll and get covered with dirt. Some of them would almost lose their clothes, and they'd fall down like they was dying. These last few years, they have got too stylish to shout.

# Stock Was Treated a Great Deal Better

*I* was born in White County, Tennessee, six miles from Sparta. No, my marster didn't have very many slaves. He had just about eight. He treated us very well. He never did whip me any. I was quite a small boy, about fourteen years old. I was seventeen when I left there. My mother, my sister, and my mother's sister and uncle was there. There wasn't much fun to be had in them times. Some of them was pretty mean. They would half-feed them and whip them, too.

They didn't have no church at all to go to. We didn't have time to study 'bout nothing but work. Sometimes we could go to the white church and set in the back. Stock would be treated better than darkies sometimes. They wouldn't whip horses half as hard as they would darkies.

We would have bacon and cornbread to eat, and sometimes on

Sundays we would have biscuits. Not every Sunday, though. Mostly we had was cornbread and buttermilk.

A bell would ring every morning for the darkies to get up 'fore day [dawn]. I didn't do much. My mother, she used to plow. I used to plow, too. The women would plow, hoe corn, just like the men would. My marster raised hogs, horses, and pretty well everything.

We had to wear tore breeches and tore shirts. Never did know what a undershirt was in them days, and no underwear of any kind, summer nor winter. Sometimes we would get some old summer breeches that was wore out, and we would wear them for underwear in the winter. We didn't have much bedclothes. Sometimes we sit around the fire all night. We could have a big, hot fire, as much as we wanted, and we would sit up sometimes to keep good and warm.

Sometimes darkies would run off and stay a good while. I was very small, you know, then, and the old folks wouldn't let me hear them talking so much. They didn't want me to know nothing about their business. We used to get whippings with a great, long hickory stick about as big as my thumb.

They didn't want us to look at a book. Didn't want us to know a thing. Didn't have no time for yourself. We would have meetings out in the woods sometimes. The preacher didn't know how to read a thing. The white folks would tell us, "Old Uncle So-and-So is going to preach to you-all today. Go down there and behave yourselves." They didn't aim for us to know anything.

The white men who had children by slaves would treat

them just like the rest. They mighta liked them a little better, but they didn't want to show it.

They didn't have no marriage contract in them days. Colored people didn't know what a license was. Sometimes Uncle Squire Wallace would go through some sort of ceremony. But he didn't know a letter in the book. Sometimes Squire would marry them on Saturday night. But ten to one, they didn't marry at all.

We all lived in the same cabin, just as many as could get in, men and women all together. They didn't care how we was treated. Stock was treated a great deal better.

It was a long time after Freedom before they had any schools. You see, the white folks wouldn't let Negroes build schools on their land.

I was in the Civil War for twenty-two months. Went in when I was seventeen years old. After colored regiment come there, they took us to town. I was with Company B, Forty-second United States Colored Regiment. We wasn't in no real fighting. We would come to a place and see that nobody would come on it. We would camp there and hold the place. We didn't allow no Democrats to come there at all. General Thomas come down here. We went to Chattanooga, Alabama, and Georgia. We would go and clean up the place and hold the places that had been taken. They was pretty sharp, I tell you something like that. One of our officers was named Lieutenant Mittie. Heap of slaves was afraid to go to the army. Everything was done when I come out. If it hadn't, I 'spect I woulda been there 'til yet. They come right in my house. I walked right out with them, never said a God's word to nobody.

Our mistress had a brother who didn't believe in slavery. He used to tell his sister [he] didn't see how she could be a Christian and own slaves. He wouldn't own a slave. He was a good Christian. Old lady was a member of the church but was as mean as you please. We never thought about anything like Freedom. My mother and father would do all their talking when I would go to bed.

I have been here in Nashville about thirty-four years. I come here with a big lumberman and worked for him about thirty years. I have been living in East Nashville ever since I come from Sparta. My son own a lot of property. He built two brick houses and sold them, and now he is building this one.

My wife was always free. She come from across the water. She didn't know what slavery was. Her mother was a slave, but her father was Scotch. She lived in White County. You couldn't tell her from a white woman. Her hair was almost long enough to touch the floor.

After I married, I went and joined farms where I was when a slave. Stayed there a good long while. I quit there and went to another man and stayed there a good while.

I get nine hundred dollars a year from the government. The fourth day of every month, I go to the bank and get my money.

# I Want to Build Up

Name unknown

*Y*es, I was a slave and knows plenty about it, but I don't care to talk about it. Nope, I don't care to give out nothing I know about it. Just don't think it would do any good. I been setting down before now and talking to some people about slavery time, and they said it was a damn lie, the white people didn't do any such thing. I was right there and looking right at it, and they was giving me the lash, too. I knows it will just start some sort of disturbance, and I don't care to talk about it. Nobody ain't goin' to believe what you say anyway. I just don't care anything for it at all, 'cause colored people don't see and use sense in anything at all. They don't do that.

These white folks here don't like to hear about how they fathers and mothers done these colored folks, and would say they were right. And these other niggers believes it, and would tell me it was all a damn lie, they never treated Negroes any such way. I don't tell them much at all. I don't want a bit o' scratch made on any book about me.

I was born in 1842, and I am ninety years this year—oldest one of my mother's eight children. There is one person here a little older than me, John Bibbs. At least, I think he is older than I am. He was good size up over me when I first knowed him.

My old marster just like the balance of the white folks. If they had to give you clothes, they would give you good ones; if it was something to eat, would give you good to eat; and if a whipping, would give you a good one. My marster whipped me once, and he told me, "Well, it won't be the last one," because he didn't give me over eight or ten licks. But the overseer did the work. He did this while he was able. He give me one lick, and I remember it now and will for the balance of my days. I just didn't want to take it.

I run away when but a chap, and when I got big enough I wouldn't stand them over me. I would fight. If I could get hold of anything, I would go to work and work like I had some sense. If he was about to get too hard for me, I would foot it. I would let him see the bottom of my heels all day. I never had but one or two that I believe could do anything with me. I commenced doing just like the men were doing. From four or five weeks is about as long as I ever stayed when I run away. I would get in your field, or somebody's, and get roastin' ears and roast them, just cook them in the shucks. When the shucks scorched enough, it would dry them out, and it was just like roasted corn. I would go by somebody's springhouse where they had their milk and help myself. This was all in Christian County, Kentucky.

I been to Nashville 'fore you was born. I was there 'fore or when the first guns were fired. I was in the battle with Hood's raiding. Nobody knows how many were killed in it. It was down on Franklin Pike. I was there 'fore the guns were fired. I came on the train from Chattanooga because Hood was so near Nashville; he had got between Nashville and Franklin, Tennessee. Men was slain from Nashville all along—all along the wayside from Nashville to Franklin. And the last gun I fired on the battlefield was at Columbia, Tennessee. They set fire to the bridge and burnt it up, and we had to put in a pontoon bridge. They got over and left some cavalry behind to keep us from putting in a pontoon bridge, but we run them away from there. We whipped around to Chattanooga because there was about seven or eight hundred of them. We had about a year and six months of this. Well, it was in 1865, but don't know what month or day. Never thought about keeping dates.

Don't know much about education. All I got, I got it out in the field. That was my fountain pen and pencil, the blade of the hoe. And my slate was the ground. What education I got, ain't a man who come in Clarksville ever seen me set in school a day. What I learnt is self-made.

My mother died just about three months before I was mustered out of service.

Me, I didn't court the girls. I didn't court them at all. All of them loved me; I didn't court. You see, they didn't do like they might do now. They would call one another "Hon," and I would say, "Sweet." And they would say, "Let's go home," and there would be something going on like a quilting, and I would go and take a gal home. They didn't do like they do now. One time, I seen a girl have her hand up in the collar of a boy, and she take a small switch off a tree—a black gum tree—and give that boy a whipping. He wasn't no-account. He had asked for her company, and she granted it. He was too young. They weren't allowed to have company before they was twenty-one years old. And for a boy when he was just about seventeen years old, he was just about the right age to be considered a man.

They would get whiskey from the still house, steal it if they got chance to do it. Me, for my part, I didn't care much about it. I heard my mother and father talking about how much they drank. My mother, she drank same as a man. I was ten or twelve years old and didn't have nothing to do with it. I heard him say, "Sally, this here will keep me warm." From what I can think of it now, I guess the snow was about a foot and a half deep. He had to go about two or three miles to a blacksmith shop where he worked, and the old man said it would keep him warm. So I thought maybe it would keep me warm, too. I didn't know nothing about it but just wanted to experience it. Folks ought to be very particular about what they do before children. I know what he said: "I will be just as warm as toast." So I wanted to be just as warm as toast.

So I went down and got that jug out from under the bed. It was might near full. Well, I got this jug up, and the strength was going up into my nostrils, and I had sense enough to know that if I didn't take it down it would go up into my nose. I drank whiskey, and in order to get it down I had to take two or three steps toward the table before I could get it down. I got drunk. I was drunk all that day and all that night. She told the white folks that I was sick, my mother did. The next morning, I was no better, and she fooled around and got a rag made of sheep wool and boiled it and poured milk down there and drenched me to death. That was to keep old Miss from knowing I had been drunk all that day. I stay drunk like today and tomorrow and like to have stayed drunk three days. She sent for the doctor, and he come. But I was just sick from being drunk, or I was just drunk and sick.

I prayed on the battlefield some of the best prayers I ever prayed in my life. Sometimes it looked like the war was about to cut my ears off. I would lay stretched out on the ground, and bullets would fly over my head. I would take a rock and place it on top of my head, thinking maybe it would keep the bullet from going through my brain, for I knew that would kill me. I'd just lay out, and I was just as thin and looked like one of these old spreading adder snakes. After a while, they would say, "Forward march." They never say, "Get up." So I'd get up myself and move off, and then they would tell me to commence firin'. Sometimes they wouldn't let me fight at all.

Our original home was in Chattanooga, but you would be called out and have to go down to Georgia and Alabama. They all join Tennessee on some part of it—Alabama, Georgia, and Arkansas. There is a little point there somewhere that they all run into one another. I believe you can go out of Tennessee into Virginia, Georgia, Kentucky, Alabama, and Arkansas.

I think it is against the race to tell about how the white people done us back in slavery. I don't want to do anything to tear down; I want to build up. These white people that used to be here before the war, it is just now and then that you can run upon them, and if you do they are about as old as I am. The law says white and black shan't mix. Now, who made that law? They made that law. I made a law with my hoe that all those weeds must die that I hit.

# They Raised the Chillun to Make Money On

I's said to be ninety-one years old. I was young when the war was going on. I was born in Bedford County. My mammy was named Mariah. She had six chillun by my daddy and three by her first husband. My missus was named Emily Hatchet, and the young missuses was Mittie and Bettie. They was twins.

We had good clothes to wear, and when we went to the table it was loaded with good food, and we could set down and eat our stomachs full. Oh Lawd, I wish them days was now so I'd have some good food. Of course, we had to work in the fields and make what we ate.

When we'd finish our day's works, our missus would let us go out and play Hide-and-Seek, Puss in the Corner, and different games.

My mammy was sold in Virginia when she was a girl. She says 'bout sixty of them was put in the road and drove down here by a slave trader, like a bunch of cattle. My mammy and two of my sisters was put on a block, sold, and carried to Alabama. We never heard from them no more and don't know where they is.

I was willed to my young missus when she married. I was young, and of course she whipped me, but she wasn't mean to me. I needed every whipping she ever give me, 'cause I was always fightin'. My missus always called me her "little nig."

My daddy could only see my mammy Wednesday and Saturday nights, and if'n he come without a pass the patterollers would whip him or run him 'til his tongue hung out. On them nights, we would sit up and look for Daddy, and lots of times he was out of breath 'cause he had run so much.

My white folks had a loom, and we wove our own clothes. I was nurse and house girl and learned how to sew and knit. My young missus was blind 'fore she died. I used to visit her once a year, and she'd load me down with things to take home—a linsey petticoat, ham bones, cracklin's, and different things. She died eighteen years ago, almost one hundred years old.

The white folks wouldn't let the slaves have a book or paper for fear they'd learn something, and if they wanted to pray they'd turn a kettle down at the cabin door. I remember hearing my mammy pray, "Oh Father, open up the doors and show us light." I'd look up to the ceiling to see if he was gonna open up something; silly, silly me, thinking such. I's belongs to the Missionary Baptist church but don't get to go there very often.

I was told 'fore Freedom that the slaves would get land, a mule, and a new suit, but our missus didn't give us a thing. She promise me, my brother, and three sisters if'n we would stay with her a year and help her make a crop she would give us something to start us a crop when we left her.

My daddy's marster was named Bob Rankin. He give Daddy a hog, some chickens, let him have a cow, her milk, and land to raise a crop on. He wanted my daddy to get us together to help Daddy raise a crop, but since my missus had promised us so much, Daddy let us stay with her a year. On the night my daddy come for us, my missus says, "I've not got nothing to give you, for I won't have nobody to do nothing for me." We went with our daddy.

We lived there on Marster Rankin's farm for years, in fact so long we thought the place belonged to my daddy. We had a house with big cracks in it, had a big fireplace, a big pot that hung on the fire, and a skillet that we cooked cornbread in. Had a hill of taters under the house. Would raise up a plank, rake down in the dirt, get taters, put them in the fire to roast. We had meat to eat in the middle of the day but none at morning or night. We got one pair of shoes a year. They had brass on the toes. I used to get out and shine the toes of mine. We called it "gold" on our shoes. We worked in the field with my daddy, and I know how to do everything there is to do in a field 'cept plow. I was always too slender to hold a plow. We had grease lamps—a thing like a gooseneck with a platted [braided] rag wick in it.

During slavery, if one marster had a big boy and another

had a big gal, the marsters made them live together. If'n the woman didn't have any chillun, she was put on the block and sold and another woman bought. You see, they raised the chillun to make money on, just like we raise pigs to sell.

I left my daddy and come to Nashville with Missus Nellie Rankin, Daddy's young missus, in 1882. I have been here ever since. I's done housework for a lot of peoples. Kept house for a woman in Belle Meade for fourteen years. Now I's ain't able to do nothing.

I's been married twice. Married Jim Ferguson, lived with him twenty years. He died. Two years later, I married George Watkins, lived with him eight years. Two years ago, he died.

I's never had any chillun. I kept wanting to adopt a little gal. The first husband wouldn't do it. 'Bout five and a half years ago, the second husband, George, come in with a tiny baby, says, "Here's a baby boy I adopted."

I says, "That is you own baby, 'cause it looks just like you."

He denied it, but even now the boy is exactly like George. He's six years old and going to school. I's got my hands full trying to raise him alone. When George died, he had a small insurance policy. I paid my taxes. I owns this home, and bought myself three hogs. I sold two and killed one. Then I got three more just a short time ago. Some kind of disease got them, and they all died.

# I've Been Here to Hear it Thunder

*I* don't know anything 'cept what happened when I was a child. I know I was born in slavery, and I know they was awful mean. I was born in 1855, and the war started in 1861. My white folks was awful bad and mean. I'm telling you what I know; they was mean. They beat us 'til the blood run down our legs.

When they left us here [after Freedom], we was naked. My sister was the weaver, and she was weaving some clothes for us, and old Mistress took that stuff off the loom and took it upstairs and hid it. We went away naked. My mother was the mother of fourteen chillun, but some died, and she had seven chillun that was her grandchillun. Their mother was the one that did the weaving.

My father was a Bailey, but Mother and Father separated before I was born. He and Mother just got mad in a quarrel and separated. He tried to get her back, and the white folks tried to get her to take him back, but she wouldn't do it 'cause he drawed back to hit her with a chair, and he'd never done that before. He woulda hit her, too, if her brother hadn't been there and stopped him. Mother was put on the block three times after that, and they couldn't sell her. They tried to bid her off for a dime, but nobody would give it. I don't know why they wouldn't, but I just know nobody would.

You know chillun get into mischief, and they get whipped for it. I often told my mother time after time that I didn't blame old Mistress for whipping us, but she didn't need to kill us; she coulda just whipped us. We didn't have on but one piece winter nor summer, and she would pull it over our head and whip us 'til the blood run down, and we was dasn't to holler. I can't remember now like I can back yonder, but I can remember that just as plain as day. We stayed there a year after Freedom 'cause we didn't have sense enough to know we was free. Some other white people told us, some that didn't have no darkies. They was glad to tell us, you know.

My mother took care of the chillun and washing and ironing, and she took me with her to wash socks and handkerchiefs. They used to keep her hired out, 'cause she wouldn't let her mistress whip her, so they hired her out and finally sold her. But she come back 'cause they said she only had two chillun and she was sound, and they found out that she had had fourteen chillun. And when she was a girl, she had knocked her toe out of place, and she was a little cripple, so they had to take her back. You know, if you sold stock and it wasn't sound like you said it was, you would have to take it back.

I seen Mistress come in there with a bucket of water to slosh on my mother, and Mother grabbed the bucket and threw it on her, and the old woman hollered murder, and all the chillun come running in with sticks and things. Then the old woman said she wasn't mad, she was just happy in her soul. One of the boys took the stick he had and hit me a lick or two, but they wouldn't let him hurt me, and he wouldn't touch Mother.

You know, that old woman was mean. When she was dying, she said she was all right, and I said to Mother, "Yes, she is all right, all right for Hell." Mother said I ought to forgive, but I can't forgive her, the way she used to beat us. Ain't no child what don't deserve a whipping. We'd eat green apples, eat dirt, and things like that, and if she caught us we would hide it behind us. And if she asked what we had, we'd say, "Nothing." You see, we done told a lie right there, and she would whip you. I'm telling you the truth. I can't lie 'cause I got to go before my God, and she's dead and can't speak for herself. But she beat me 'til the blood run down to my heels.

Mother said when she was sold she had a baby in her arms, and her other boy next to the baby was standing by the fence crying. When she come back, she had me. I was her baby.

My aunt, she'd slip meat skins through the crack to us chillun 'til that hole would get right greasy; she had a little hole in the floor that she could use. And we would go down to the orchard and broil them or cook 'em some way. We'd put the little ones in the henhouse, through the hole they left for the hens, and they'd come out with an apronful of eggs, and we'd take them out to the woods and cook 'em some way. And we would steal chickens, too. Me and Sister Lottie was the biggest ones in the bunch, and we was real little. The white chillun would help us eat 'em, too, and they would go to the house and get salt, you know.

When my mistress would whip me, I'd squall and squall, and she'd shake me and tell me to hush. Then I'd just jump. I had to do something. I'd go round back of the chimney and cry easy.

My mother never did whip me over twice, and I would mind her. I was 'fraid of her, and I always did what she told me. She was part Indian, you know. I said to her after Freedom, "It's funny you wouldn't let Mistress whip you, and yet you let her whip us chillun all the time."

She said, "If I'd started that, they woulda sent me away, and I never woulda seen you no more."

Yes, when we left there, we had our dresses pulled round in front to hide our nakedness. Many's the time I had to ask the white chillun for bread, and they'd slip and get us bread, and meat, too.

God, my deliverer! I despised her. One of her daughters was dying, and I was going to a picnic, and Mother said, "You ought to go by and see Miss. She's dying." And I told Mother I didn't want to go. But you know, I had been brought up to obey, and I was grown, but I never could tell her I wasn't going. I just left like I was going in that direction, but I went on where I was going, and I never did say no more to

Mother about it. When we was little, she used to whip us and then make us kiss the switch. She was the meanest one of the daughters.

I'm seventy-seven now. I've been here to hear it thunder.